BERKELEY JOURNAL

Jesus and the Street People
—A Firsthand Report

BERKELEY JOURNAL

Jesus and the Street People
— A Firsthand Report

CLAY FORD

Harper & Row, Publishers
New York, Evanston, San Francisco, London

CONTENTS

CONTENTS · vii

Acknowledgments

I appreciate the opportunity I had to work in the Berkeley street culture as a summer missionary; this was made possible by the First Baptist Churches of Pomona and Berkeley and by the American Baptist Home Mission Society. I also appreciate the support I received from the faculty and administration of the American Baptist Seminary of the West at Berkeley and at Covina.

I wish to thank Mary Williamson, a secretary at ABSW, Covina, who typed the original manuscript for me.

I especially wish to thank Cheri, my wife of several months, who typed the edited and revised manuscript and whose suggestions and insights have been most valuable.

I thank Berkeley and its inhabitants for friendships, insights, and experiences that have profoundly affected my whole life.

And, most importantly, I thank Jesus Christ my Lord, who loved me and led me and was present with me as I worked in Berkeley. It is to him that I dedicate this book.

Introduction

I was one of four volunteers sent to Berkeley, California, in the summer of 1970 by the American Baptist Home Mission Society to work with the First Baptist Church, Berkeley, in the "Telegraph Avenue Project." The Berkeley street scene is something I had seen before. Three days after my graduation from Davidson College in North Carolina, I made my way to Berkeley where I studied for two quarters at the American Baptist Seminary of the West. Although I was in fairly close contact with the street culture during that period, my contact was of a relatively superficial nature. The life-styles of the street people were radically different from any I had seen before, and it took awhile to adapt to my new environment. There were many things I could not understand about the street people: why they were so dedicated to drug use, why they were so bent on destroying the Establishment, how they could read the filth and hatred in the underground newspapers, why they dropped out of what I had considered to be productive lives.

After living in Berkeley for ten months, I transferred to the American Baptist Seminary of the West at Covina, California. My decision to leave Berkeley was made on the basis of academic concerns rather than on the basis of location and opportunities for ministry, and I left entertaining the hope that I would some day return and get involved in the street scene. While working at a church in Pomona, I heard about the "Telegraph Avenue Project," quickly applied for the position and was accepted.

Anticipating a very enlightening and exciting summer experience, I decided to keep a journal, recording notable events, encounters with interesting people, and reflections on various theological, political, and philosophical matters. This little book is the result of that decision. I might add that a few changes have been made in the way of clarification, some of my ideas have been slightly revised in light of new insights and experiences, and many of the names mentioned here have been changed for obvious reasons.

The Telegraph Avenue Project ministered to the needs of the Berkeley street people through three programs: a free coffee house, a meals program, and a runaway center. Our headquarters was the basement of the First Baptist Church of Berkeley, where there were facilities for all three of our assigned programs. The location of the church was excellent; being one block west of Telegraph Avenue and three blocks south of the Berkeley campus of the University of California, it was at the heart of the Berkeley street culture.

There were four summer missionaries—Donna, 20, from Colorado; Chuck, 20, and Gail, 17, both from Pennsylvania; and myself, 24, a seminary student at Covina, California.

The pastor at First Baptist, Berkeley, who was overall head of the Telegraph Avenue Project, was Dr. Ray Jennings; his assistant was Fred Keene, a U.C. graduate student and a church deacon.

Having dedicated my efforts to Jesus Christ, it is my hope that his spirit may use this book to further his cause and purposes in a sick, suffering world.

CLAY FORD

Let the words of my mouth,
and the meditation of my heart,
be acceptable in thy sight, O LORD,
my strength, and my redeemer.

(Ps. 19:14, *AV*)

BERKELEY JOURNAL

Jesus and the Street People
—A Firsthand Report

1 · Kids Hung Up on Drugs and Sex

June 15

It didn't take me long to get into the swing of things. I wandered up to the U.C. campus and sat on a low wall at Sproul Plaza. A big guy, about 6'6", with long black hair and beard, approached me, grinning weirdly. I thought for a moment he knew me, so I looked intently at him to see if I recognized him. He just stared at me. I realized that I did not know him and turned my head in another direction, wondering what sort of problem this guy had. He was standing no more than a foot from me staring down with piercing eyes. He spoke, asking if I minded talking to strangers. I returned my gaze to his face and looked at him bewildered. Then he said, "Why don't you and me go over there [pointing to a spot where there were no people around] and talk." I asked him what he wanted to talk about. He responded, "Oh, it will come up when we talk about it." I realized then that he was most probably a homosexual and I was a prospective pickup. I looked at him and said, "No." I tried to appear more confident than I really was. He kept staring at me while I began to look around uncomfortably at other things. Finally, I looked him square in the eye and said, "No," again, very emphatically this time. Eventually he walked away.

After this encounter, I knew I had been initiated into Berkeley life once again.

As I had driven into Berkeley today from Covina I was apprehensive. I have been Interim College Minister at a church in Pomona, where my job has been quite different from what I will be doing this summer. In some ways this summer's job is much more to my liking: more freedom to spend time with people rather than program, not the hassle over dippy things, not the politics prevalent in a large church. On the other hand, the work here will be with an entirely different kind of people—kids hung up on drugs, sex, and who knows what else, as compared to kids who have grown up in the church and who are at least nominally Christians. Whereas there had been no real fear of anything in that job, this summer's job is very dangerous in some respects. The Berkeley street culture is infested with sickness, violence, and paranoiac distrust of "straights," one of which I appear to be.

2 · Terry

June 16

Chuck, one of the other summer missionaries, and I will be moving into a vacated sorority house tomorrow. All we will have to do for free rent and kitchen privileges is keep the doors locked and sprinkle the lawn.

I saw a guy named Terry whom I knew when I was going to school in Berkeley. I think he's twenty-seven years old now. He was in college at one time but dropped out with only three units short of a degree. Says he couldn't see any reason to get it—he had learned what he wanted to know. I think part of the reason for his dropping it was that psychological pressures became more than he could handle. He's been receiving welfare because of psychological incapacity to hold a steady job. For the past several years, he has lived here in Berkeley, trying to get himself together. For awhile he was taking drugs, but he's given that up for more serious attempts to find meaning in his life.

Terry is now involved with the transcendental meditation movement. He says it really helps him have peace of mind. Terry is authentic—he wears no masks. He is good-natured, quick to smile, has a sharp wit. He's the kind of guy you like to see, to chat with about what's happening. Though he does have some psychological problems, they appear only from time to time, as storms on an otherwise calm sea. His usual disposition is very warm and sensitive; his personality radiates acceptance and peace.

But Terry does have a sore spot. He gets unglued when Christians try to convert him, and many have tried. Believing in the relativity of truth and, therefore, of religions, he resents anybody with the attitude of "This is the way it is," though he himself is like that when it comes to talking about transcendental meditation. I think a large part of his resistance is due to the Christian sexual morality, which, if he became a Christian, would require quite a transformation from his present habits.

I told Terry about the homosexual who tried to pick me up as soon as I got into town. He recognized the description I gave and he told me he is one of the leaders of the Gay Liberation Front in Berkeley, an organization that is trying to free homosexuals from the oppression of social condemnation and discrimination. I told him I agree with their cause to the extent that I feel they should be treated as human beings; however, I said, homosexuality negates rather than encourages true fulfillment of one's sexuality.

While I was walking on the campus today, a girl tried to collect bail money from me for persons in jail arrested for walking nude in the streets. A member of the Nudist Liberation

Movement, she believes that if everyone in the world would go nude, many of the world's problems would disappear. She seemed attractive, intelligent, and even level-headed. I was amazed to see a girl like her in this particular bag. It is really strange how people get caught up in such causes; there are many more worthwhile ones this girl could have chosen.

The Hare Krishna group, dressed in their pale yellow robes was on the campus giving out incense sticks and chanting "Hare Krishna" to different beats. The name of the movement is The International Society for Krishna Consciousness, Inc. Their only means of support is contributions, and so, along with the stick of incense they give, comes a request for a contribution. You get to keep the incense whether you give money or not, but if you don't give money, they have designed a subtle facial expression that makes you feel about as low as an earthworm. The purpose of their chanting is to arrive at a consciousness of the presence of God, thus bringing about a certain radiance and peace of mind. Most of these people appear to be gentle and kind, but I saw a few lose their cool under harassment.

3 · The God Squad

June 17

We summer volunteers, jokingly calling ourselves the God Squad, had meetings today until 3:00 P.M. We met with Dr. Jennings and Fred Keene for a general orientation and for assignment of specific responsibilities. I have the responsibility for the coffee house with Gail assisting; Donna is in charge of the food program; and Chuck is working on the street to make contacts for the runaway center. Although these are our specific areas of responsibility, we will each work in all three programs. After our general orientation, we met with Rev. Dick York, head of the Free Church in Berkeley. York has a radical theology, possibly because he was pushed to it by public opinion and police harassment. The Kingdom of God in his theological framework means the "liberated zone," or the structure that comes into existence after the overthrow of the Establishment. When I asked him if destroying this particular "world pig" would not just result in another "world pig," he agreed but said he felt we should join the revolution and humanize it. "Pig" has the same bad connotations describing the world power structure as it does when used to describe a bad policeman. It connotes unfairness, exploitation and oppression of the weak, racism, impersonality. I asked if he thought it would be inconceivable or futile to try to humanize the existing "world pig" rather than replace it. He answered that that was a much harder way of doing it. York is a very sharp, articulate person. He graduated from seminary a couple of years ago and has been ordained.

Our next meeting was with Bill Crawford, a retired Army medic who now works at the Berkeley Free Clinic, which is located about half a block from the church. The Free Clinic treats street people with drug problems, cuts, and venereal diseases, as well as anything from psychological problems to warts and toothaches. Crawford is a black man with graying hair and beard. He is a warm, dedicated man, but also firm, and he doesn't seem to be the type who enjoys playing games.

Our final meeting was with Margo Horn, the young woman who is the only fulltime staff of the runaway center. She filled us in on the operation of the center and gave us a brief training session concerning the alternatives open to a runaway kid seeking guidance. Our primary function is to help runaways understand the courses of action open to them, and allow them to arrive at a decision on their own. The alternatives open to the runaway are: one, contact family and go home; two, turn himself in to juvenile authorities (one kid actually did this—to get back at his parents!); or, three, be placed temporarily in a foster home with parental approval. Over 65 percent of the kids coming in for counseling end up going home. Margo's job is much more difficult than I imagined. A great deal of the difficulty lies in the strain generated by trying to win the trust of both the street culture and the police department. Trying to play by the rules of both cultures is frustrating.

4 · "Hello, Is this Satan?"

June 18

The meals program at the church is getting a boost from street people who are volunteering to work in the kitchen. One of the volunteers is nicknamed "Satan" because of his flaming orange hair and beard and his ferocious temper. Satan is organizing the other volunteers for work. He says he wants to help in the kitchen all summer.

Satan was on the job in the kitchen today when a man came to see the pastor in his office upstairs. The man was a classic example of the Prodigal Son. Having run away from home at the age of fifteen, now after seventeen years he wanted to return to his family. Since he had no money he did not want to go back to his parents having to tell them he was broke. The pastor was impressed with the man's sincerity and believed that he had finally found himself and was ready to begin anew. Ray wanted to give him ten dollars. He found he had only five in his billfold so he told the visitor he was going to call a friend downstairs (meaning Donna, Chuck, Gail, or myself). Ray later described to us the very appreciative expression on the man's face as Ray dialed the number of our phone in the kitchen. It is easy to imagine what was going through the visitor's mind, "What a fine Christian minister . . ." Since Satan was the person nearest the phone when it rang, he answered it, and the pastor asked, "Hello, is this Satan?" Ray told us that when he said this the man in his office just about fell off his chair.

After lunch I went to the University of California campus and listened to an argument between a tall, silver-haired Christian woman with an eight-year-old kid and a black guy who was resisting conversion. The black man had been performing for the small crowd gathering around, and I guess the lady was aware of this; however, she was using his performance to attract the attention of passersby to her rhetoric about sin and salvation. The eight year old was amazing in his ability to speak and to use logic and in his knowledge of the Bible. But in a sense I feel sorry for him, because the theology he has been taught is hopelessly rigid.

The woman was saying that since this black guy was not a Christian, everything he said and did was Satan in him. She implied that human beings have two alternatives: they are either puppets of Satan or puppets of God. I got a headache just listening to the conversation so I went across Sproul Plaza to the steps of Sproul Hall.

I hadn't been there long when the homosexual I met earlier came up to me. Once I had established the fact that I am not homosexual and that I knew he did not want involuntary participation in homosexual activities, I felt at ease. He is a very large guy, does not seem effeminate at all.

We talked for about forty-five minutes. The purpose of his movement, the Gay Liberation Front, is to oppose the oppression binding homosexuals in our society. Homosexuals want to be open about their activities and not be forced to hide that part of their lives, nor be made to feel guilty about it. He questioned my position, so I told him I was a Christian and that I believed the Bible to be a source of truth inspired by God.

God created man and woman, I said, as I began explaining a Christian view of sexuality. He gave them sexuality that they might reproduce and that they might become one, both physically and spiritually. Since God intended the sex act only for a man and woman in a lasting relationship characterized by love and fidelity, then conformity to that relationship encourages fulfillment. If a sex act changes God's intended use of sex, I continued, that act negates fulfillment. Though I can accept a homosexual as a person whom God loves and as a friend, I told him that his homosexuality inhibits the positive development of his human personality. I added, however, that I feel the neurotic view held by some who believe sex is bad or dirty can be every bit as dehumanizing as homosexuality. Once he discovered the biblical-Christian framework of my thought, he realized that we have different basic assumptions. But he would not be persuaded that homosexuality could destroy the development of his personality.

My attitude toward a homosexual is the same as my attitude toward other human beings; his life is sacred to God, so valuable to him in fact that there is no limit to what he would do to make the homosexual whole. God does not force himself or his healing power upon us—that would be unjust, a violation of our free will. All we must do is respond to his love, shown to us in Jesus Christ. The essence of sin is rejecting God's purposes and his sovereignty. By rejecting him, we alienate ourselves from the source of fulfilling love, the source of *real life*, which is communion with Jesus Christ, living in the love of God. It is my calling as a Christian to conform my attitudes to attitudes that are worthy of God. To the extent that I am successful I will love the homosexual and hope that some day he will be free and whole.

I'm infatuated by a girl I met. Elaine is a college graduate with a Master's Degree in French, age 25, on the move. Her beauty is not so much physical as it is an inner beauty reflected by her warm eyes. Her eyes also reflect the deep suffering she has experienced, which may be connected in some way with a nervous breakdown she had while in college. She, like so many sharp college grads nowadays, is on the road, looking for some place to plug in. With her liberal antiwar political views she cannot identify with the Establishment. During the past year she has lived in states ranging from South Carolina to Kansas to California. Maybe she has found "home" now.

5 · Cheyenne

June 21

I've been playing cards a lot in the coffee house with the street people who come in. Some of them have genuine honesty and goodness. One of these is Cheyenne, the most striking person I have met so far this summer. Cheyenne is black, wears a poncho, a hat, and a large earring in his left ear. He is about 22, a college dropout, and he has been in the service. Now Berkeley is his home.

Cheyenne grew up in a tiny town in Georgia, where he says the most exciting thing to do was to hike to the big highway and watch the cars go by. His father was a preacher, but unlike many preachers' kids, he wasn't forced to go to church if he didn't want to. He says he went a lot anyway, because he wanted to.

One day Cheyenne went out to the big highway and hitched a ride, leaving behind his small town, his family, and a style of life to which he has never returned. He made his way to Kansas where he met a group of guys with whom he felt at home. They were members of Christ's Patrol, an organization of Christian motorcyclists who ride together from town to town with the purpose of proclaiming Jesus Christ and the new life he offers. Cheyenne still carries a little Bible with him in his shirt pocket. In his billfold he has papers from somewhere declaring him to be an ordained minister.

Cheyenne is hard not to love. His smile is warm; his laughter is alive and contagious. He is always ready to believe the best about people. He is a friend. He knows what it means to hurt inside, so he avoids hurting others. Playing hearts he tries not to let the other players get hurt by getting too many points. Often he will take the Queen of Spades himself, rather than give it to a person who is already losing.

Cheyenne has a deep need to be liked, a need so strong that it sometimes pulls him to do things he knows he should not do in order that he gain the acceptance of his peers. A look into his eyes reveals years of suffering, self-contempt, and searching for love. He has Jesus in him. But unlike Jesus, sometimes Cheyenne crucifies himself. He wanders over the moral borders separating his real convictions from the general moral convictions of the street culture. He often goes along with the street culture's view of sexuality, and, as long as the girl is willing, he will generally go ahead.

The toll of cheap sex has taken its effect on Cheyenne; it causes him deep inner conflicts; it makes him unable to respect himself. He is such a beautiful person, yet he is thwarting his own fulfillment. His lack of love and respect for himself lead him to take drugs on occasion, though he doesn't seem dependent on them. Often he joins in the revolutionary rhetoric against the Establishment, but his heart doesn't seem to be in it. Speaking about racism one day, he told me that he never notices the color of a person's skin but looks on the heart. His life witnesses to the truth of that statement. His goodwill and fellowship are given to all regardless of color or life-style.

Beneath their wildly and weirdly decorated exteriors of multicolored clothes, hats, ponchos, earrings, and long hair, the street people are genuine human beings in search of someone who will love them, show they care; and also in search of an opportunity to love, to care for someone or something themselves. Many have serious drug problems, problems with sex, difficulty relating to other people. The majority are bored with life, empty, just passing away the time on "the Avenue," perhaps secretly longing for a time when reality will grab them by the heart and say "Here I am." Quite a few are hassled by the police regularly; almost all who have been here for any length of time have been arrested for one thing or another.

The overwhelming majority, perhaps all of them, have had experience with drugs more dangerous than marijuana. Drug use is not a rational thing; reason has nothing whatever to do with one's decision to try it. It is more a consequence, I believe, of spiritual starvation, an attempt to stand in the light, to leave the darkness. It is a trip to the light where life and its meaning are clearer but perhaps still inexpressible. It is a substitute for the real thing that negates the possibility of having the real thing, which is a relationship with Light and Truth that is not a trip but a lasting habitation. Drugs provide a trip away from the futility, emptiness, and darkness of life to the light; but there is no functional relationship between this light and the life they temporarily leave. A relationship with God is different than a trip in that it brings clarity and meaning into all areas of one's life. It is not a trip *to* the light but an existence *in* it; that which appears meaningless acquires meaning, despair becomes hope.

A trip to the light involves no responsibility; existence in it *means* responsibility. Life comes to mean total responsibility to God and to our neighbor; but it is a joyful responsibility, for by accepting it we are fulfilled.

6 · The Jesus People

June 22

I'm writing while sitting at Sproul Plaza on the campus of U.C. Berkeley, which is only three blocks from the First Baptist Church. Across the plaza is the Student Center and to the left is a crowd listening halfheartedly to Galen, one of Berkeley's street evangelists. Hubert, the most popular of the evangelists here, just finished his preaching about twenty minutes ago. Hubert is a seminary graduate, from Kentucky, I believe, and is about 45 or 50 years old. He is a colorful individual, short, with red hair and freckles and a missing front tooth. Ever-ready to jump up on a chair, a wall, or anything else available, he harangues all the "Godless wretches" and "miserable filthy-hearted sinners" that will listen. He smiles half-lovingly and half-condescendingly during these assaults on their "dirty hearts," and I suppose it is his contagious grin that has kept him not only alive but actually well-liked by most of those who hear him.

Hubert is a very popular person in Berkeley and succeeds in drawing large crowds to hear his proclamation. I am not sure at all, however, how successful his efforts are for the Christian cause. He draws people to himself but often alienates them from Christianity with some of his questionable interpretations of the Bible, his failure to see Christianity as involving more than just the spiritual dimension of life, and his conviction that he no longer sins since he was "cured" of all sinful tendencies. In spite of these facts, I find myself loving him as a brother; he has guts and his efforts are sincere.

Before I began writing today I was listening to a conversation between two couples, with Hubert preaching in the background. One couple were members of the Christian World Liberation Front, an evangelistic street oriented Christian group in Berkeley. The Christian couple were not offensive, dogmatic, or condescending. Their attitude was that of persons sharing something beautiful and valuable with friends. There was no falsely generated enthusiasm, no sugarcoating of Christianity to make it appear a perpetual bowl of cherries. So often that kind of approach is misused. The person sharing his faith often lacks confidence in what he says. Christianity has not really become deep enough or real enough in his life; consequently he feels the need to generate an enthusiasm of his own, and he often sugarcoats Christianity to make it more acceptable. There was no trace of that approach in this conversation.

I was particularly impressed with the girl, whose name was Laura. Her eyes reflected the love and "humble confidence" that only the spirit of Christ can give. Laura and Steve went through something similar to the "Four Spiritual Laws" booklet printed by Campus Crusade for Christ, an evangelical student movement begun by Bill Bright, a Christian businessman. The four laws stated briefly are as follows: (1) God loves you and has a plan for your life; (2) man is sinful and separated from God, thus he cannot know and experience God's love; (3) Jesus Christ is God's only provision for man's sin; and (4) we must individually receive Jesus Christ as Savior and Lord; then we can know and experience God's love and plan for our lives. These little booklets are used sometimes as the tools of spiritual scalp-hunters, but it was refreshing to see Laura and Steve use it well. Many times the person talked to becomes an object, not a person; there is no real concern or real communication. But the medium is the message: the person representing Christianity becomes the message of Christianity. Words of love mean nothing if there is no love conveyed in the interaction. There was love in this interaction. Laura and Steve made a positive impression. They were not primarily concerned with making converts, as one who puts notches on his belt; they were concerned with sharing their Christ with persons they cared about.

The couple they talked to were straight rather than hip, probably Cal students; they were intelligent and not ready to accept anything they could not understand. They listened seriously, their response was not hostile, cynical, or close-minded. They could detect in us (I eventually became involved in the conversation also) something they were glad we had found—inner peace. They asked the usual questions, why is there evil if God is loving and all-powerful, what happens to those who don't hear about Christ, why is Jesus the only way, aren't other religions just as close to God?—all good questions. We answered them as best as we knew how. The fellowship was enjoyable and warm. Both of them remarked how they enjoyed talking with us. They left with greater openness to the love and spirit of Jesus Christ.

Theologically, the Christian World Liberation Front is radically different from the Free Church. CWLF is primarily an evangelistic group. Its members stay almost entirely out of the political controversies in Berkeley. They believe, basically, that "Christ is the answer," which I feel can be a terrible oversimplification. Certainly Christ is the ultimate answer, but the answer to many questions, though ultimately in Christ, must be put into action by his followers.

A Christian might give a tract to a starving child, or to an illiterate immigrant seeking unsuccessfully for employment. But paper isn't very nourishing food, and a tract doesn't teach a man how to read. To the CWLF members, however, justice seems to have nothing to do with Christianity, and those who strive to promote it are attacked with the idea that if everyone were converted, there would be no injustice. Are the oppressed to wait for the conversion to Christ of all the oppressors? Is that the only hope Christians can offer them? I often wonder how so many Christians who take the Scriptures seriously get around God's absolute demand for justice. They must be blind; or, if not, must cut several hundred passages of the Old Testament and many parts of the New Testament out of their Bibles. Many well-meaning Christians pride themselves that they are Bible-teaching, Bible-believing people. They should become Bible-doing people! Preach the gospel—that is only half the commission. The other half is to live it. God demands our love for him and for our neighbor. Can we love our neighbor if we don't care how he is treated by other people? Does not love mean more than friendliness? Can you love without working for justice?

Jesus Freaks, or Jesus People, are found in growing numbers in Berkeley. They are turned-on, enthusiastic Christians and are not timid in spreading their faith. Many of the Jesus People here were former street people in the drug scene before they came to know Jesus Christ. However, quite a few in Berkeley this summer are straights; some are college students from other states here only until school starts in the fall.

Their evangelistic approaches differ. Some of them pass out Christian tracts in the streets to passersby, asking them if they've heard the good news about Jesus Christ. Some work behind the scenes, on a person-to-person basis; others like the excitement of large crowds and do most of their witnessing where the action is. Sometimes they carry signs like "One Way" and "Christ is the Answer" at the end of political marches. Their activities range from preaching on the steps of Sproul Hall on the U.C. campus to picketing nude bars.

The good traits of the Jesus People are much more numerous than their bad ones: they are usually joyful and alive; many are bubbling with love. They are quick to smile, and even quicker to share their faith in Jesus Christ. They are morally and physically clean, and their language bears witness to those truths. Life *means* something to them, and they are eager to see other people experience the abundance of life they have found in Christ. The Jesus People are similar in appearance to the rest of the Berkeley street people, but their life styles are radically and excitingly different.

Though most of the Jesus People have attractive personalities and are assets in the Christian cause, some of them do become offensive. The most common offensive traits are a self-righteous dogmatism and the unwillingness to treat the opinions and beliefs of others with respect. These traits cause quite a few arguments in Berkeley.

Many of the Jesus People are new Christians. They make mistakes; in their joy and enthusiasm they are often insensitive to the feelings of those with whom they talk. They can become dogmatic; they can get messed up on far-out, ridiculous interpretations of God's Word. They can absolutize their own experience and exclude as invalid the experiences of others. They can hold tight to "truths" which they find out later to be untruths. They can overemphasize the importance of lesser gifts like speaking in tongues and ignore the more important gifts and fruits, like prophetic preaching, love, long-suffering. They can be so overjoyed about their newfound spiritual life in Christ that they fail to see the practical implications of what it means to love one's neighbor. They can become so engrossed in the study of prophecies regarding the second coming that they don't have time to minister to the suffering world around them, and they can be so convinced that the second coming is soon that they are too heavenly minded to be of any earthly good. I know these traps for new Christians firsthand; because I tripped through most of them myself.

In spite of my reservations, I am convinced that the rise of the Jesus People, both here in Berkeley and elsewhere, is the result of God's working in our midst. Only the Spirit of God can free from the addiction of heroin, the terror of acid flashbacks, and the insatiable lust for sexual gratification that ignores the cost to self and the other. Only the Spirit of God dwelling in one's very being can give a person peace in the midst of turmoil, joy in the midst of despair, love amidst hatred and mistrust. The

Jesus people have a lot to learn, but then so do I. My calling is the same as theirs, to love Jesus Christ and obey him as Lord. To the extent that Christians—be we members of establishment churches or the Jesus People movement, Pentecostal or Catholic—are true to this calling, we will be truly one, as God intends.

The Free Church goes the route opposite that taken by the CWLF. It comes close to being a left-wing political organization, ministering only to the physical needs of the street people. Whereas everything in the CWLF is influenced by an otherwordly orientation, the Free Church is interested only in this world. Jesus Christ, their proclaimed liberator, is being used for their cause, I am afraid, rather than using them for his. The Christian faith has validity only to the extent that it suits their purposes. And, as Judas did, I fear they will betray Christ in the end.

Of these two radically different groups, I am unable to identify myself completely with either. I am evangelical in that I believe Jesus Christ is alive, he is the Lord of history and to know him personally is eternal life. I am social-gospel oriented in that I feel Christians should actively oppose all dehumanization, be it personal, political, economic, or social. God's love is a love that includes the whole man—body, mind, and spirit. Marxists and secularists operate as if there were no spiritual dimension to man, or to life. Some of the Jesus People operate as if fulfillment is not influenced at all by living conditions, education, or nutrition. Faith without works is no better than works without faith. Evangelism without love of the whole person is just as incomplete as social action without any concern for the spiritual dimension of man. *There is a tremendous need today for a balanced Christian faith.*

Around me I hear harmonicas playing, people chattering, an occasional scream, dogs barking, the buzzing of machinery tearing up the pavement on Telegraph Avenue, the buzz of motorcycles and the whirring of cars going down Bancroft Way. I like watching people go by. One particular aspect of Berkeley

I'm not really used to yet is the bra-less girls. It is all a part of the movement to be liberated, I guess, and the movement has extended even to body parts, i.e., breasts traditionally oppressed by straps. I have rather mixed feelings about the situation. As a 23-year-old male, I enjoy looking. Saturday I was sitting at the plaza with the other summer missionaries and a large number of other people listening to some guys playing guitars and singing, a frequent occurrence at Cal. A beautiful bra-less girl dressed in blue jeans and a skintight, long-sleeved top began to dance. She was a very graceful dancer, and her attire made her all the more enchanting. To be honest, I was fascinated by her—by her freedom to dance, to do her thing. On the other hand, to see such a girl, so enticing, arouses in me feelings of passion and lust which I have learned through experience, painful experience, are incompatible with the Spirit of God. To give way to lust and to impure thoughts opens the way for impure attitudes which sooner or later manifest themselves in actions.

7 · Alabama

June 25

Sometimes I talk with people at the runaway center, trying to enter their world to a certain extent. Often that world is frightening. There are some pitifully sick people in Berkeley. Anywhere else these people would probably be picked up and taken to some sort of institution, but in Berkeley they are left alone, sometimes terribly alone.

One runaway I have met is 16 years old, a girl with red hair and freckles. She is so hungry for love that she grasps for it, and when she receives it she becomes a clinging vine. She claims that her home life was so terrible that she attempted suicide (slashed wrists, I think) just to get out. They took her to the state mental hospital. She ran away and tried to go home. She says her mother called the police, so she went next to Berkeley. I try to help her, because I care about her, but it is very difficult; when I enter into her world my mind begins reeling, and I actually get very dizzy.

Berkeley is not a refuge only for young people; older folks who have been crushed by life end up here where they melt into the scene and while away their hours of misery. There are some older women here—usually very alone, very cautious, perhaps paranoid. Some are long-time alcoholics; others are involved with drugs. Everywhere else these people would be frowned upon; at least in Berkeley they are not considered to be worse than anyone else. That does not mean they are loved or befriended; it means only that they are not condemned.

One woman in particular stands out in my mind. She looks to be about 50 years old and has graying hair that is always in curlers. Her hair is filled with lice. She always carries a large bag and sometimes two or more little ones. I think she has a cookbook in her bag, along with some papers and bits of food she picks up here and there and saves for hard times. She also has a dog which she leads on a leash. This woman has been totally crushed by her experience of life. She trusts nobody except perhaps her dog. She takes drugs to drown her misery; her face is wrinkled from terrible strain. Her eyes are distant; they often do not see what is in front of them but make their way to some far-off world where life is not such misery.

Paranoia is widespread in Berkeley. So many con artists, so much pushing, double-dealing, saying one thing and meaning another, especially when the subject is money. I saw two guys operating on Telegraph Avenue. One of them was going through some kind of fit—it looked convincing. His eyes were glazed and bulging; he was groaning terribly, but I'm sure it was a put-on. The other guy was asking for money so he could take him to the hospital. Everyone who didn't give was made to feel like the lowest and most depraved of human beings. The con man looked at those who passed by with bitter contempt and disgust. I imagine they make lots of money like that.

This conning and outright deception does not occur quite so much among closely knit groups of friends, but between strangers and unrelated groups. Among the street people high value is placed upon individual honesty within groups of friends. To betray a friend is perhaps the worst of crimes. However, anything one does outside the group is okay; or, if not okay, at least not a cause of serious rebuke. This seems to point to a very important fact: people need people; they thirst for meaningful relationships more than anything else, unless they are addicted to something. Without these close, meaningful relationships, life loses value and despair creeps in. Despair is a killer.

Sometimes I talk with people and ache inside. A guy from the deep South named "Alabama" has started coming to the coffeehouse. He is fairly nice-looking, tall, has a small beard and sideburns. The first time I saw him, a week or so ago, he was sitting very still on the counter by the sink in the church kitchen. He had assumed a strange yoga-like position, with his hands pressed together at the middle of his chest, his elbows pointing straight out, and his legs crossed. His eyes were wide open and appeared somewhat glazed. I went up to him and looked into his eyes. No response. I snapped my fingers in front of his face; still no response. I turned to someone and asked, "What's with him?" As the person answered that he was practicing yoga, Alabama came out of it, whatever it was. He claimed he had not seen me or heard me snap my fingers in his face. I still don't know whether I believe him or not. He says yoga helps him by giving him peace of mind.

Alabama and I were talking a couple of nights ago. He was telling me how he was going some place to have sex relations with a girl and how he got sidetracked and ended up having sex relations with another girl instead. After laughing heartily about this and other of his sexual conquests, he began talking about his drug experiences.

He said he thought he would start on speed again. I asked him if that would not mess up his mind. He said, "No. See, what I do is stay on speed just for a while and before it can mess my mind up, I switch to acid, heroin, or something else. Then after I've been on them awhile I go back to speed."

Alabama then related to me how he got in trouble in Texas one time for cursing a Texas state senator who backed into the car Alabama was riding in. He was arrested for disturbing the peace, obscene language, and, he claims, impersonating a human being.

His conversation rambled on until he started talking about his home and family in Alabama. He told me he grew up on a large farm in the South; his family is upper-middle class and attends church. He really misses his "mumma." He hasn't been home for a year or so. Now that he's 22, he feels it's time to be on his own. The impression he's given me is that the reason he's a street person here in Berkeley has nothing to do with radical politics or rebellion against the values of his heritage. He is living for pleasure, escaping the responsibilities of adulthood for as long as he can. He is here because he wants to be; rather than being alienated by the society, he has alienated himself from it. He himself has chosen to be lazy, irresponsible, and degenerate.

Then Alabama started telling me about his little sister. "Yeah, she's twelve years old, coming right along. I send her joints once in awhile. I been thinking about going home pretty soon cause I think she's ready for a tab." A tab is L.S.D. I suddenly got a very pained expression on my face. I guess he took it to mean that I doubted that his sister was really groovy enough at twelve to handle acid. He said, "No she really is ready; I'm serious." Man, I just wanted to shake this guy apart. I was filled at the same time with disbelief, anger and compassion. Compassion for him because he believed so sincerely that giving his little sister a tab of L.S.D. was sending her out in the right direction; compassion for his little sister, whose life he was very probably going to ruin. I was just about to say something when he asked, "Have you ever had acid?" I said no. He said, "I suppose you get high on J.C., huh?" I said yeah. I decided to hold up on my assault on his attitude toward sex and drugs with the hope that I could share Christ with him, dealing with the root of his problem rather than the symptoms. I told him about the love of Jesus Christ: seeds were planted.

8 · Reaching for the Hand

June 26

Many young people today throw out Christianity because of the history of the church in America as a protector of the status quo; because Christian doctors build half-million dollar houses and think their faith extends only to individual relationships and good work; because Christian businessmen smile and go to church on Sunday but play the cutthroat game of capitalism all through the week; because white churches justified slavery and still, in many cases, close their doors to blacks; because some churches operate as if capitalism is part of the Christian faith. I cringe when I have to identify myself with Christianity as it has been manifested in much of American history: exploitation in the name of Christ, killing in the name of Christ, hatred in the name of One who knew only how to love.

But I thank God that I can identify with Jesus Christ, that my life has its meaning in serving and following him, living in his presence and love. He gives meaning to all my activities, to all areas of my life.

Christianity is not the history of the church, nor is it a set of creeds or standards; it is not knowledge of God through philosophical syllogisms. It is knowing God as a loving Father, leaning on him, trusting him, basing one's life on his existence and his will. It is being motivated by his love, being guided by his will. It is a real relationship with the Creator whose creatures we are. Jesus Christ is the hand of a loving Father, reaching down to his sick, rebellious children, pleading that we take his hand and be made well.

9 · Freedom at Thirty-Eight Dollars

June 27

Cheyenne was arrested the other day. The police had a warrant for him. It seems he had $38 worth of traffic fines last year which he did not pay. He had no money and was put in jail. If he did not come up with the $38, he could have been fined $500 as well as spend some time in prison. Some of the others were talking about it at the church, wondering how they could get the money to free Cheyenne. I went down to the jail and paid the fine. It was a pleasant surprise to realize the money does not really mean as much to me now.

I tried to bail him out anonymously, but it did not take long for him to discover who got him out. I wanted to do it anonymously because I did not want Cheyenne to feel as though he was obligated to me, and because I did not want everyone who happened to get arrested to think that I was going to bail him out. But Cheyenne I love, and I am glad I paid his bail. It may be one of the only breaks he has gotten in his life. To see his happiness to be free again made it worth every bit of the $38.

10 · Sam and Smith

June 28

I was worried when we opened the coffee house that I would not be able to break through the personality defenses the street people carry with them to protect themselves in their harsh surroundings. But playing hearts with them has helped a lot. The atmosphere of the game helps the drop-ins relax and open up.

Sam, one of the friends I've made playing cards, is a professing Communist. Sam is now over 40 years of age. Originally from Canada he came to this country when he was 17. Fired up against the fascism of Hitler, he joined the army. He acquired a medical discharge, but during the Korean War he waived it and joined the Air Force. He was an electrical and explosives specialist. Sam became sick of the abuse of rank and power in the service. His ability made him invaluable but his habit of exposing the corruption he saw kept him from being promoted. He came to see the Korean War as "none of our business" and therefore became anti-American. He is equally opposed to our involvement in Vietnam.

We talked one night about injustice—exploitation of the poor by the rich, racism, pushing drugs. Serious Communists, I've learned, are every bit as opposed to drug use as Christians but for different reasons. For Christians, human life is sacred and drugs are destructive to its development. For Communists, drugs keep potential party members and leaders from effective participation in the Revolution. Communists are against drug use by Communists; Christians, if they really love their neighbors, are against drug use by everybody.

Sam and I can agree on what is wrong with this society. Our disagreement emerges in our highest loyalties and our methodologies to correct social evils. His highest loyalty is the Party with its fallible leadership and ludicrously flexible dialectical process which can be used to rationalize any action the Party wishes to take. My highest loyalty is the living God, who has revealed himself to me in the Person of Jesus Christ. I am guided not by the methodology of historical materialism or the dialectical process, but rather by the will of God as revealed in the Bible and through his Spirit which has been real to me since I became a Christian two and a half years ago. Christians are limited in their methodology whereas Communists can justify anything they do, so long as it is working toward the overthrow of the capitalist system and the establishment of a Communist society. Sam feels the only way to rid the world of greed and the evils of capitalism is to destroy all the greedy people, all the capitalists. The Christian cannot join hands with the Communist, for he must value the life even of the oppressor. The Christian knows that God is, that he is Lord of history, and that his will is love structured around justice. And he knows that God has the power to transform the relative "No" into the absolute "Yes." So the Christian must do it as he sees it, being influenced neither by the right nor the left but by the Word and Spirit of God.

Sam usually seems to be genuine, honest, and sincere. He believes he is right. Provoking him by questioning his opinion on something like American foreign policy causes the bitterness and contempt of America within him to rise from the depths of his soul. Sam, according to his own testimony, was married and had five kids. His wife was mentally disturbed; he claims she fed him sexually depressant drugs in his food during a period when she had extramarital relationships with two local policemen. One night Sam says he caught his wife with one of them. He got a gun and almost shot the man but he stopped: he did not want his kids to grow up knowing their father had killed a policeman. He wishes now he had killed him.

He became filled with rage; his wife divorced him on the grounds of insanity, I believe, and he lost his five kids in the process. He has not seen them for eighteen years. Time has not healed Sam's wounds but has apparently served to make his hatred deeper and more intense. Sam's hatred runs much deeper than his apparent warmth.

Sam is a regular at the coffee house. We play cards together a lot. He works hard, sweeping and mopping the floor, fixing faulty electrical equipment. He works almost as hard as the four of us summer volunteers, yet he doesn't get any pay. (We get $100 a month.) I believe a part of his helpfulness is genuine appreciation for friendship, free meals, and a place to play cards. Another part is that I demonstrated a trust in him. He asked if I would go with him sometime to buy a two-dollar switch for a broken coffee percolator. I said I would give him the money and he could buy it when he had time. He came through and I got change back.

Sam is an evangelist. He is out to win people for his faith just as I am out to win people to mine. He sees in me a prospect. He knows I see injustice as he does; but what he does not know is the depth and strength of my commitment to Jesus Christ. By his friendship, loyalty, and example, he hopes to bring me into the fellowship of his comrades. By my friendship, loyalty, and example, I hope to bring him into the fellowship of Christians. I pray for his very being, for his salvation. Salvation? Yes, salvation from a life based on half-truths and illusions, motivated by the self-defeating desire to destroy. And salvation to a life motivated by love, its meaning found in conformity to the will of One who transcends all relativity but yet is involved in that relativity, in whose kingdom we who take his hand will live forever. Heavy.

Another of my coffee house friends goes by the name of Smith. He is white, tall, slender, 23 years old. He's a fairly good-looking guy with short black hair, a mustache, and a little beard. His dress is not out of the ordinary (actually, there is no "ordinary" in Berkeley), except for a brown leather hat he wears sometimes. The hat has three leather strips about a foot long streaming out the back and they sway in the breeze as he walks. On the end of one of the leather strips is secured a round piece of metal which Smith keeps as a weapon in case he doesn't have time to get out his razor blade.

Smith grew up in an upper-middle class family in New York. His father owns a chain of paint stores and seems to have provided Smith with everything his heart desired. Smith is still a spoiled little boy in many respects; he has the most incredible pride I've ever seen. When he wants something like food, for example, and when it's not yet time to eat at the church food program and he is told he cannot have it, he explodes in violent rage. One night something petty came up and he shoved his fist through a glass panel on the kitchen door. The door was opened and against the wall; his fist went through the glass with such force that it kept going and made a fist-sized hole in the kitchen wall!

When Smith was fourteen years old, he stole a car. He said the keys were in it, and he wanted to have some fun. He didn't intend to keep it, though. His dad got things squared away for him. He later stole three more cars on different occasions, but his father was somehow able to keep him out of rehabilitation institutions. Consequently Smith never learned to be responsible himself for his own actions. He didn't learn that he couldn't just do what he wanted and expect to get away with it, that "good old Dad" wouldn't always be there to get him out of trouble.

As a Marine Smith saw action in Vietnam a couple of years ago. During his third year of four in the Marines, he deserted. He got fed up and could not take it any more. The "Yes, Sir," "No, Sir," and taking orders finally got to him, so he left. He was caught and arrested. At his trial, something the judge said set him off, so he cursed him. He angrily described the situation to me: "I ain't gחnna crawl for no judge." Consequently he received six months in the Treasure Island brig (from which he escaped once but was caught within twelve hours on Telegraph Avenue), and also a Bad Conduct Discharge. A B.C.D. is the worst you can get. It is almost impossible to get a job with one of those on your record. The sad thing is that he actually seems proud of it.

Smith is very cautious with the girls. He has a great deal of pride and is slow to commit himself to anybody for fear of being rejected. This does not mean that he abstains from sex; he is just careful to see that there are no commitments.

He wears a Mao button, but his interest in Communism is not as serious as Sam's. It seems to be more a result of his boredom than anything else. I overheard him say, "I hope there are some good riots; it's getting boring around here." He takes quite a bit of acid, and one of his favorite pasttimes while high is staring at the blood vessels in his arms. He has an explosive temper, a deeply violent nature, and, apparently, an empty life. He seems to have a great deal of potential, but in the Berkeley street culture he is learning few if any constructive ways to develop it. His biggest problem is that he has no motivation. He has absolutely nothing to live for. I know of only One who can solve that problem for him. It is my hope that I may soon call Smith "brother."

11 · I Had Masks but No Face

June 29

Cigarettes are bummed all the time in Berkeley. Cheyenne,

Sam, and Smith smoke all that they can beg, borrow, or steal. It is perfectly acceptable here to ask total strangers for cigarettes, and for a street person to be turned down in his request, if the person has more than one left, is almost a crime. I have even seen people jump out of a car at a red light and ask the driver in the next lane for a cigarette.

I am sure, if I smoked, I would have to give away at least twenty cigarettes a day. I used to smoke over a pack a day. It was really getting to me; during the early part of my senior year of college, there were mornings when I woke up at 5:00 A.M. gasping for breath. I felt I had to quit, but it seemed an impossible task. I even went to the extreme of telling my college friends if they saw me smoking, I would give them $5. They let me off every time. This situation led me to a significant experience in my life which gave me my first real evidence that there is a God and that he has power. In self-disgust and anger, while alone in my room, I yelled at God—not really sure he was there —"God, if you are for real, I want to quit smoking. What good are you if you can't help me?" I had no more cigarettes for the rest of the day. However, that night my room seemed to be filled with smokers, two of whom were my roommates. Unable to stand it any longer, I asked someone for a cigarette and I smoked it. As I smoked it I began getting a strange sensation; I watched myself put that smoking white tube into my mouth and thought how absurd the whole thing was, especially since it was doing me nothing but harm. That was the last cigarette I ever wanted. My desire was broken, I was free.

I knew at that time that God was real. It wasn't very many days after this experience that I committed my life to the Christian cause. Of course there were some other circumstances and reasons leading me to this commitment.

I grew up with middle-class values. Work hard, do good, excel. In my home town of 20,000 I was a big shot. I was elected president of my class every year in high school; I played football and basketball, golf and tennis. I had almost an A average in school, was active in many school organizations, and was in the senior class play. I thought I was where it's at—being popular, being an officer, getting a long list of honors and achievements I could carry along with me.

I sold Bibles for a company in Tennessee for the two summers following my freshman and sophomore years at Davidson College and made over $5,000. Selling Bibles gave me insight into human nature; I learned a lot about people, what makes them tick. I became interested in human psychology and decided to major in it. I wanted to find out what life was all about.

The second effect of my selling experience was that it turned me into a role-player. I could play just about any role in order to make a sale. I could be a pious, solemn young man or a raucous, fun-loving hell-raiser—whatever the particular situation I was in seemed to warrant. One day I awoke to the realization that I had no real understanding of who I was or what my life was all about. I had many masks but no face that was really me. I was empty, and for awhile I resigned myself to the notion that life is absurd and has no meaning.

My grades began to drop; my once responsible attitude deteriorated; my moral standards collapsed. For two years I was on a downhill trek toward complete worthlessness. I lived for parties; I boozed it up; I became a smooth-talking playboy. Life was a silly game. I came to see the futility of working hard when you have no reason or purpose for which to work. I experienced the difficulty of trying to motivate myself to study and to be responsible about things when my life had no direction or meaning.

At the end of my junior year at Davidson in North Carolina I came to an important decision. I decided that life must have a meaning, and I became determined to find out what that meaning is. I was taking a course on basic Christian beliefs that semester taught by a professing agnostic. At the end of the semester we were to write a "credo"—what we believed. Most students wrote elaborate theologies; I turned in four pages, handwritten, saying I was a role-player, empty, in search of life's meaning. I wrote that I had heard somewhere that Jesus had said, "I am the light of the world." Although I didn't know exactly what this meant, I interpreted Jesus to be saying that he knew what was happening, that somehow he was the key to the meaning of life. I wrote that I thought this might be true, and that, although I didn't know in what sense it was true, I was determined to find out. I meant what I said.

The first semester of my senior year of college, I took a course on the life and ministry of Jesus. Jesus was a figure that attracted me in a strange sort of way. As I read the books of Matthew and John in the Bible, the person of Jesus Christ never ceased to amaze me. He was completely loving but also as strong a man as I had ever imagined. The way he handled himself and the things he said all intrigued me. He seemed to believe that he was somebody extremely important; he spoke with authority that rested not in worldly status but in something else. He didn't feel the need to prove himself, but his mere presence seemed to be enough for most to realize that here was someone special.

I thought about the impact Jesus made on people. He said, "Follow me," and men followed him. He didn't bother to explain his program or why they were to follow. He didn't have to. Those words, coming from him, were enough. He had power. Two things in particular impressed me about Jesus. First, he came across real; he played no roles; he knew who he was, what he was about, where he stood. He was totally authentic. Second, he, with no apparent weakness, gave himself to those who were weak. He took upon himself in love the burdens of those unable to handle them themselves. He gave himself away.

Jesus became my hero. I didn't believe in the miracles or the resurrection or anything like that at the time, but I knew that here was a man who seemed to know what was happening. As I continued my study of this man Jesus I became more and more infatuated by him—his love, his strength and boldness, the power of his personality, his authenticity. For awhile I toyed with the idea that he was crazy: a man who comes across like Jesus does in the Gospels is either telling the truth or he is crazy. The claims of Jesus about himself and his purpose were so radically distinct from the claims of other men about themselves that he could not have been wrong about himself and his mission and still have been sane. Yet Jesus didn't seem to me to be insane. He was too authentic, too convincing. He seemed to be grounded in a truth much greater than any truth I had experienced myself.

I became thirsty to know more about Jesus. Perhaps I became obsessed with him in a sense. I felt as though I was a man who had been traveling in a desert, thirsty, moving closer and closer to an oasis, not knowing for sure whether what he was seeing was a mirage or not. But I became convinced as I got nearer that this was no mirage; Jesus was really an "oasis." He was for real. My thirst to know Jesus Christ became the most important purpose of my life. I wanted to lift him up out of the Bible, fall at his feet, and worship him in awe and adoration.

I had no close Christian friends nor was I affiliated with any church or Christian group. I talked with no one about my search. It was all on my own, by myself. Right before the Christmas holidays I read a book by Rudolf Bultmann, *Jesus and the Word*. He describes the teachings of Jesus. Jesus wasn't saying believe this, or do that: he was saying, "Commit your life to me, give yourself to me, follow me. It's either-or, yes or no, paint or get off the ladder."

Without realizing what was happening I committed my life to follow Jesus Christ. I did not know he was alive, that he had actually risen from death. That seemed ridiculous to me, a legend perhaps built up about him by well-meaning followers. But something happened when I committed my life to follow Jesus Christ. He made himself real to me. The Person of Jesus Christ stepped out of the Bible and into my life. His love engulfed me; the power of his presence transformed me. I became aware of a whole new dimension of life. I came to know a personal God, a God who is a loving Father. My life had meaning. It made sense now. I was a child of God, responsible to him and for every human being.

The transformation this new awareness brought about in me was amazing. I changed so quickly that it was all I could do to adjust. Everything looked new and different. It was frightening, but in an excitingly beautiful way.

In April of my senior year at Davidson, I decided to become a Christian minister. I got the "go-west-young-man" spirit and left for California three days after my college graduation. Since that time God has become even more real to me. His love never ceases to amaze me. Though my life as a Christian has not always been easy or carefree, it has always been deep, fulfilling, and real.

12 · The True Polarization

July 1

Young people are beginning to do in the open what the Establishment does in secret. They are perhaps closer to God in that they are not hypocritical about what they do. But they are crucifying themselves, and their death is just as inevitable as those against whom they rebel. There is nothing fulfilling about either L.S.D. or liquor; there is nothing about cheap sex that promotes love and justice, whether it takes place in the open or in private; there is no healing power in violence and hatred, whether it is directed by the Establishment or toward it. The injustice of pushing acid on kids is no less ugly than the injustice of job discrimination. Dealing in drugs is no less disgusting than selling faulty used cars.

Often I am critical of the Establishment, and I believe rightfully so. But to be honest, I have to even the score. The percentage of hypocrites, liars, thieves, and cutthroat capitalists is no higher in the Establishment than in its opposition. The self-righteousness of many of Berkeley's so-called revolutionaries is repulsive. Some of them are honest and sincere people. They are out to overthrow a system they believe is irreparably evil. They are seriously committed to the destruction of the Establishment for ideological, political, humanitarian, and perhaps even religious reasons. They take life seriously, and they believe they are doing the right thing. These are only a few.

The majority of them do not really care that much. They live life as though it is an absurd, silly game, screwing up their minds with drugs, crucifying themselves and other people with sexual misuse and exploitation. They are playing games as we all did when we were ten-year-old kids—games like cops and robbers, hide and seek. The games they are playing now are undoubtedly more exciting, but for most, it is still just games. Screaming obscenities at little old ladies and breaking store windows, stealing things they don't need and provoking the police to lose their cool are the games the revolutionaries play.

They scream for justice but do not get too upset when eight girls were raped in Berkeley during the past year or when two seven-year-old kids were allowed to get hooked on smack right in front of their noses. Justice grows out of the rightful regard for human life; it is directly concerned with how people are treated by other people. It is hypocrisy to want justice for groups of people and not care about individual persons. Injustice is corporate—this is what the Establishment fails to see, or fails to act upon if it does see. But it is also personal—and the anti-Establishment fails to see or to act upon this.

I am not defending the Establishment. It is comprised of many who have the false idea that the American way is the Only

Way, ordained by God. Members of the Establishment rationalize the existence of ghettos and poverty by projecting their own guilt to "those bums" who are just "too lazy to work." But, generally speaking, the majority of the anti-Establishment is no more just, no more righteous, no more serious about doing right than the Establishment.

The Right Wing and the Left Wing are equally wrong. Collectivism is no more fulfilling ultimately than individualism. The Right sees a polarization between Communism and the free world; the Left sees a polarization between the world pig and the people. But in a broader, deeper context, the true polarization is between those who love and those who do not; those seeking justice, unity, and reconciliation and those who are not; those who have a reverence for life on both individual and corporate levels and those who do not. In the context of the true polarization, those of the Right and the Left who are motivated by fear and hatred are actually on the same side.

God sides with neither the Right nor the Left. He sides with persons in the ranks of both, persons who seek his truth, thirst for his will, and lean on his power and guidance. He is on the side of those who love and seek to do what love requires of them. He sides with those who are oppressed and those who seek justice. Concern for law and order without equal concern for justice is abomination. Peace at the price of justice is a hideous crime. God is Redeemer, but he is also Judge. His willingness to forgive must be seen in the light of his demand for repentance.

13 · Mark

July 5

Mark came into the church four days ago for one of the free meals. He wanted to talk to a Christian, so he was directed to Ray, the pastor, and to me. As I was the first to come around, he talked to me. Mark is nineteen years old. He has lived away from his family since he was fifteen. He finished about a year and a half of college before he dropped out. Mark has been very lonely; he has been crushed by a family that says there is not enough room in it for him any longer. He is a fine-looking person, strikingly similar in appearance to Paul McCartney of the Beatles, only Mark has longer hair and fewer clothes.

Mark said he had been a serious Christian for about five months. There was an intensity about him that is very difficult to describe; as if he had an enormous burden on his shoulders and needed to share it with someone. He is soft-spoken, has a certain tenderness and warmth; it pains him to see people hurt, physically or psychologically, probably because he knows the agony of suffering himself.

We began talking about the Second Coming of Christ. I had just bought a book entitled *What Jesus Said About It*, a helpful little book that arranges all the teachings of Jesus under topics. Since I had it with me at the time, we turned to "Judgment" and read all there was in it about the Second Coming.

We read how people would come saying, "I am the Christ," or "Lo, he is here," or "Lo, he is there." And we read how we were not to believe it, because he will come in such a way that every eye will see, like lightning that streaks across the sky from the East to the West. We read also about events that would take place before his coming—famines, earthquakes, wars, and rumors of wars. Mark asked if these had not all taken place and I answered in the affirmative. He then said he believed the end was near.

I told him that the Apostle Paul thought it was near in the first century and Martin Luther thought it was near in the sixteenth century. I told him although I firmly believed it was coming, I did not believe it was necessarily coming soon, though I did not discount it, for it will come as a thief in the night. He looked pained for a moment, then spoke very quietly but firmly: "It is coming very soon. I mean, I *know*, I know it is."

We looked at each other for about fifteen seconds without speaking. God works in strange ways. It is not impossible that Mark could *know* something I did not know; God could have shown him things he has not shown me. Mark went on to explain how he had prayed and fasted in the mountains for many days by himself; how he felt called by God for a special mission. He explained how things had taken on a double meaning. Everything he saw, read, and heard about was being used by God to teach him spiritual truths.

Mark spoke very gently and quietly; but he spoke with a certainty that convinced me he was either sick or telling the truth. I said in regard to the Second Coming that it made little difference to me if it was in my lifetime or not. If it is—okay, I will be with Christ; if not, I will still be with Christ. And its coming should in no way affect how I act, what I am, what I do. Our motivation as Christians does not come from our knowledge that the Second Coming is soon. Our motivation comes from our love and trusting obedience to our Father who has redeemed us.

As we talked, Mark began to loosen up. His profound intensity began to give way to joy. He had found in me a friend, someone with whom he could communicate, someone who could understand, even if I could not agree. He said that I was the first person he had met who was willing to do God's will regardless, explaining that this was an intuitive thing. He seemed to see in me a person to whom God had led him, as if I was an important piece of God's overall plan for his life.

The praise he heaped upon me was in great part due to the fact that he had been terribly alone and I had befriended him. He was in need of more than friendship; he, like so many other wandering youth in Berkeley, has no place to stay and usually ends up sleeping on rooftops, in parks, or on floors of buildings he can get into. I offered to let him stay in the inside yard of the sorority house Chuck and I are living in. I had every intention of letting him stay in the house, but I first wanted to see what Chuck thought about it. Also, I did not want any of the regulars at the coffee house to know I was letting someone crash there. Then they would want to also, and there's no telling what might happen if we opened it to everyone. We have explicit instructions not to let any visitors stay; however, I felt Mark was especially in need of my friendship as well as a place to stay, so I made the decision and was ready to take the consequences.

That night after work, Chuck, Mark, and I went to our house; we talked, listened to music, drew portraits of each other. Chuck went to bed; Mark and I stayed up talking. We began talking about drugs, and this is when I began to sense that he was more than just a little mixed up. He felt that the mind-expanding drugs like mescaline and L.S.D. make people more aware and that God has put them here for that purpose. He got the absurd notion somewhere that the passage "Timothy will be with you soon" in one of Paul's letters speaks to us today and that the Timothy referred to is Timothy Leary, the ex-Harvard professor who has become an L.S.D. fanatic.

I disagreed angrily at this point. I have seen minds screwed up and lives ruined by drugs. You cannot effectively cope with reality if you are not even in touch with it, but live instead in a fantasy world of moving dots, curving lines, colored lights, and worthless hallucinations. Mark argued that everything good has its bad points. I argued that often bad things had aspects that could make them look good.

14 · Trouble Breaks

July 7

Rioting shook Berkeley on the night of the Fourth. The righteous spirit of revolution was nowhere to be seen. It was vandalism pure and simple. One hundred and fifty windows were broken on Telegraph Avenue. The police were supposedly caught off guard. By their not being around, however, there were no screams of "police brutality" to justify the riot.

Dick York of the Free Church was walking with his wife on the night of the Fourth; he had no part in the riot. Two men pulled up in a car, chased him, and beat him until he was unconscious. He is still in the hospital. It is rumored that the police department refused to listen to a complaint about the incident by a black man who is on the City Council. It is things like this that cause me to move farther to the left: the stupidity of the Fourth of July spree of vandalism moves me to the right. I have no idea what side I will be on in the Revolution. Probably neither.

Yesterday began about 11:30 A.M. with the doorbell ringing furiously. Chuck went down to answer it a few seconds before I did. When I got there Chuck had already let the person in, and they were in the bathroom. Chuck came out with a shocked expression. He started jabbering something about a girl. I went in to see what was going on. In the bathroom was a very pretty blonde who was a member of the sorority whose house we were

using; she had been by a few days earlier to pick up some mail.
I saw that she had been slashed on the face with a knife. A deep
gash cut across her lip; it was clean so it did not bleed much.
Some guy she did not know came up to her as she was getting
into her car and jabbed her with a knife. Not even realizing she
had been cut, she began running and since our place was the
closest place where she knew anyone, she ran to us.

I wanted to rush her straight to the hospital. When she talked
the gash spread apart. But she thought it would be better if she
went first to where her father works, since he knows the doctors
and the insurance regulations. So we took her to see her dad.
He was panicky: for a split second as he looked from his daughter's mouth to us, I saw in his eyes the urge to kill. It was a second
of potential murder. But it passed as she explained that we had
helped her. Apparently his mind was not clear, because he
decided to take her to the police station first and then to the
hospital. I asked nonchalantly, "You are going to take her to the
police station first?" He said yes. He seemed to care more about
revenge than he did about the recovery of his daughter. I did
not question him further.

After this incident, I returned to the house because I do not
have to be at the church now until coffee house hours. Mark
called me. He wanted to know if he could stay with me that
night. He said he needed to talk, as he was having problems
with his mind.

The other night during my conversation with Mark I began
to worry seriously about his sanity when he told how he took a
quadruple dose of mescaline. He said that he had done it for
God and had asked God to change him into a better person
through the experience. He described to me his sensations. He
felt a tremendous amount of heat, as if his mind had melted.
While on this trip he said he saw himself "in an earlier life dying
on the cross." He paused and I looked at him for a moment, not
sure whether or not to ask the question that was on the tip of
my tongue. I asked it: "Mark, do you think that you are Jesus

Christ?" He paused. "Yes . . . Yes, I do." I was silent for a full thirty seconds, searching his face, his eyes. For a moment my mind wavered on the brink of insanity; I let myself move into his being, feel his feelings, think his thoughts.

He and I were alone in the silence, looking into one another's eyes. The meeting of our beings took place in the sphere of the between. For a moment it was almost possible for me to believe he was the Christ come again. He was so sure, so convinced—but so sick. I told him I did not believe he was Christ; I told him I loved him, that he was my friend, but that I thought he was wrong. He reluctantly admitted that possibility but he said he hoped that we could still be friends and work for God together.

The following day Mark came off it and let go of his illusion. Ray found him crying in one of the meeting rooms of the church. I talked with him, trying to be an anchor in the midst of the chaos and insanity around him until he could get himself together again.

On the night of the Fourth Mark had gone up into the hills to get away from the impending riot. He went with two friends, Carla and Bill. Carla is a small sixteen-year-old girl who has been a patient at a state hospital because she tried to commit suicide. She will not live with her family, and her family will not allow her to live in a foster home. So, tragically, she has ended up in the jungle of mass insanity which is the Berkeley street culture. Bill is a Black from Louisiana who has been here for only a short time. He digs Carla and, according to her, protects her in the daytime so he can sleep with her at night. She is afraid of him, and with sufficient cause. He has a serious drinking problem and was a boxing champion somewhere at one time. After quarreling with Carla and Bill, Mark ended up leaving his companions and sleeping alone in a small restroom somewhere. Mark told me simply that his mind started acting strangely and so he left them and decided to return to Berkeley the next day.

It was upon his return yesterday, right after the incident with the girl who got cut, that he called me, wanting to talk and to know if he could sleep at the sorority house that night. I was a little hesitant, but finally I said he could stay. Here was a person in great need of a friend and in need of a helping hand. So I said yes, ready once again to accept the consequences of my decision. Little did I know what lay ahead.

I talked with Mark for hours yesterday at different times. Ray talked with him a great deal also. Ray had called Mark's family a few days earlier because Mark had indicated he wanted to go home. His father is one of those men of high principles who places his principles above his son. His family has no room for him anymore; it was out of the question. Ray broke the news to him.

Law is based on principles. But the purpose behind the law is love of human life and protection of that life. To withhold love from a person in need of it for the sake of principles is a great mistake. Such was the mentality of the Pharisees 2,000 years ago, and such is the mentality of many of America's "God-fearing decent folks" today. Adherence to principles is better than nothing. But it cannot heal; it cannot give another person a reason to be alive, a reason to hang on to the realm of sanity.

As Mark and I talked, my mind traveled back and forth across the border separating his world from mine as though I had one foot on solid ground and the other in quicksand of fear and despair. Mark felt that God hated him and wanted him to burn. He cried repeatedly that he was the worst person in the world and was convinced that God was determined to destroy him. I calmed him down and prayed aloud to God for him. He started sobbing and we hugged each other. He said he did not know what he would do without me.

I knew now that he needed help that I could not give him. The strain of the situation was really beginning to get to me, but I was determined to see him through. I was not going to betray him. I began talking to him about his need for help. I suggested that maybe the state hospital in Napa might be able to help him get his head straight, that perhaps his problem was just a chemical imbalance, that he would get three meals a day there instead of just one, and that once he got himself together he would be better able to serve God. We talked to Ray about it. We all agreed that we would go the following morning.

Because of rumors that Telegraph Avenue was going to be leveled with fire bombs by "the people," it was suggested that we close the coffee house early. But Fred said he would stay until 11:00 P.M. and keep it open, because he did not want those in the coffee house to go up to Telegraph. He stayed, and Mark and I went to the house where Chuck was listening to music.

The three of us went to the kitchen where we were going to have hot Ovaltine. As I was preparing it, Mark said he was tired and asked if he could pass on the Ovaltine and get some sleep. So Mark went upstairs while Chuck and I stayed in the kitchen and talked as we sipped. We talked about how many weird things had been happening, about the senseless violence that takes place in Berkeley. We talked about our past sweethearts: about the girl he went with for four years and whom he broke up with just before leaving for Berkeley, and about the girl I had once been engaged to. Then the conversation drifted to the psychic, the mysterious, and the gory. We talked about dreams people have had, some of which have come true. I told him I had had two dreams that something frightening would happen to me this summer, but that I had not taken them seriously or let them affect me until quite recently when I saw how close danger, even death, is to anyone in Berkeley. Someone could cut you for no reason, shoot you, beat you, rob you without any provocation. In our conversation we exaggerated the dangers of Berkeley, but in light of the events of that day, it did not seem exaggeration in the least.

We began to sense that something was wrong. My mind returned to Mark. Chuck and I stood up at the same time and went upstairs. Mark was not in my room in the extra bed I have there. Our thoughts raced to other parts of the enormous sorority house. We got a flashlight and began to check every room on the second floor, even the closets. No sign of Mark. I figured he had left the house. But Chuck and I were shook. We were not about to go to bed until we knew where Mark was. We proceeded up to the third floor and opened the door. Immediately we smelled the smoke. We went down the hall, turned the corner, and there was Mark, standing in his underwear. He watched us as we walked toward him, a wild look in his eyes. "I didn't have the guts to do it," he said.

He had a started a fire in a corner room and in the hall. He set his pants on fire and some sheets, trying to burn himself. Apparently when he heard us looking for him (Chuck had yelled his name over and over again), he had put out the fire. He burned both hands and one leg and foot, not seriously but bad enough. He said, "You want me to burn, don't you? God wants me to burn." Chuck and I assured him of the contrary. He responded, "Well, *they* do." We asked him who he meant by "they." "The people," he answered. "They want to drown me, behead me. Why, Clay, why do you want me to die?"

I told him that I did not want him to die, that I loved him and wanted only for him to be well. Chuck and I were able gradually to calm him down. Then we helped him to get dressed.

We called Ray who was still at the church. Ray, Fred, and Beth, the pastor's daughter, picked us up at 1:00 A.M., and we all went to Herrick Hospital. They treated Mark's burns as a psychiatrist talked briefly with him. The psychiatrist's prognosis: chronic thought disorders; only a very slight chance of ever living a normal, productive life. He said that Mark could probably be brought back to health in a setting where people genuinely loved him, treated him as an adult, and had lots of time over a long period to devote to him. He went on to say that meaningful relationships, people to whom he could turn who cared, were his best hope.

In the first years of his life Mark did not have the love or the security that would have enabled him to develop and adjust to reality. Instead he was driven by loneliness, lack of love, and despair to build his own reality in which he was somebody who mattered; indeed, in his own fantasy world he was Jesus Christ, the Lord of life. His experiences with drugs had melted his mind in such a way that he could no longer differentiate between reality and fantasy.

The hospital where we took Mark has ambulance service to Napa State Hospital, but since Mark wanted us to take him, we decided to drive ourselves. We got home at 4:00 A.M.

Today I have been trying to get in touch with the woman in charge of the sorority house for the summer. I am going to tell her what happened and that I take responsibility for the damage done. The carpet is burned both in the corner room and out in the hall; there is a burn in one of the mattresses; and there are four burned sheets. I still believe I had no choice: I just could not turn him away as he was.

Thousands of Marks are roaming the streets and hillsides of America—some young, some not—all starving for love, for someone to be real to them, for someone to care. Reaching out into nothing over and over again causes people to build their own little private worlds in which they really are somebody. Only love, constant love over a long period of time, can bring them back to the real world.

Even so, sometimes I wonder if Mark is any worse off than many of the so-called sane people. Life is a jungle for just about everyone in the streets of Berkeley. Often it is a fulltime job to stay sane in mass insanity, to be able to lend a helping hand rather than need one. God is my anchor, my strength, and my hope. His love keeps me going.

15 · Asked to Leave

July 10

Chuck and I were asked to leave the sorority house. The people who manage the house were not nasty, but the customary warmth shown us was lacking, and I guess understandably so. Fortunately I have a friend at the Baptist Seminary in Berkeley and I am staying now in the men's dorm. Chuck is living for the time being with Fred. We will have to pay for damages, though I do not know how much yet—perhaps around two hundred dollars. It is good to have friends: Ray, Fred, Chuck, Donna, and Gail have all volunteered to help out with the repair bill.

16 · Love and Pain

July 13

I operate on a deeper, more personal level now than before. I'm sure it's partly because I've become more adapted to life here in the street culture. I have let my hair grow out and am growing a beard and mustache. I look less straight than I did, and that has helped me relate more personally with many street people. For the first two or three weeks some of them thought I was a narc (narcotics agent) or an undercover cop or FBI agent. Now they have greater trust in me and know that my bag is the Christian ministry and not "busting the people."

I've grown as a person and as a Christian. I am more able to put into practice what I profess, namely, to love. I have really grown to love the street people, not that I agree with their life-styles, attitudes, or ideas. And not because they are particularly lovely people, for most are not. Yet I have come to love them just the same. And along with this love has come a deep suffering. When you love someone, it hurts to see him get his life messed up—by someone else or by his own wrong decisions and actions. I think of Jesus, how he said he came not to judge but to save, and how, when asked by the Pharisees why he had fellowship with sinners and outcasts, he responded, "Who needs a doctor but the sick?" I am gaining a fuller understanding of Jesus this summer. I shudder when I think of the suffering he went through because of those he loved. His love is so deep, so strong; my suffering for these street people I have come to love is but a scratch I'm sure in contrast to the deep gash in his heart. But it hurts.

To see people you love melt their minds with drugs, or crucify themselves spiritually and emotionally by giving away their bodies just to alleviate a drive or pass the time, or watch them become controlled by the cancer of hatred and paranoia, or see them wander about empty inside with the constant companions of frustration and despair—man, it hurts!

I am in pain particularly because of Cheyenne. He is in jail again; this time his bail is $6,000 and that is more than a little bit out of my range. The story is that he was caught breaking into a store and stealing a pair of pants.

Cheyenne didn't need the pants. He has some clothes, and he also has enough friends around, including myself, that if he needed a pair of pants, he could have gotten them without stealing. Cheyenne is basically a good-hearted and honest person, and stealing isn't typical of him at all. He and Smith had a job a week or so ago that lasted a few days. They worked with some other street people for a contractor who was tearing down an old school building about two blocks from the church. The foreman had to leave one day, and he put Cheyenne in charge. One of those working tried to steal something, and Cheyenne told him to cool it. Cheyenne got threatened and almost got in a fight, but he didn't back down. He usually takes responsibility seriously and is honest.

Cheyenne has a strong need to be accepted by his peers. And I am convinced that this is what caused him to blow it. He had been spending quite a bit of time with Smith, Sam, and a guy named Mac, a 23-year-old alcoholic and college drop-out from Pennsylvania.

Smith and Sam are both negative influences on Cheyenne— Smith, because he cares nothing about life at all and is generally destructive for the heck of it; Sam, because he is filled with hatred for the "capitalist pigs" and is adept at inspiring others to conform to similar attitudes. Mac is usually good-natured, the Walter-Mitty type, always dreaming about some thrilling adventure he is going to have some day. As it turned out, it was Mac who inspired the idea of stealing some clothes in the first place. He talked Cheyenne into going with him on this Robin-Hood-steal-from-the-rich-give-to-the-poor type mission; and wouldn't you know it! Mac got away and Cheyenne got caught. What a bummer. Smith and I and Mona, a girl from Chile whom Cheyenne likes, are planning to go see him soon at Santa Rita prison.

17 · Few Evidences of Love

July 15

I've been surprised since I got to Berkeley at how few times

I've heard the word "love" outside the context of Christian fellowship and street preaching. I'm even more surprised at how few evidences of love there are in the street culture. The street culture is anything but a loving community. Love and trust are only empty words. Yet never have I seen such a need for these realities.

18 · Suffering Love

July 19

At the beginning of last week a black dude named John came to the coffee house to see me and Gail. He said he appreciated what we were doing for "the people," the free food and coffee house, and that he wanted to help us out financially. He offered to bring in a band called "Daybreak" to play for a benefit dance. Since our funds are rapidly diminishing, we agreed to the idea. As it turned out, however, our dance was more a benefit to John than it was to us. Gail gave him ten dollars for publicity as an initial investment, and he also wanted 25 percent of the money we took in. Gail paid another eight dollars for food and refreshments, and the "free" band ended up costing us another ten dollars which they needed to pay for the sound equipment they had rented. The gross take was $24, of which John got six, the band ten, leaving us eight. Gail had invested $18, so we went about ten dollars in the hole. Chalk it up for experience.

Actually the financial loss was not the real catastrophe that happened Friday night. At about 11:20 P.M. a big fight broke out. Since I was in the kitchen when it began, I know what initially happened only from the stories of those who saw it. Some black guy, known particularly for starting fights, I was told, started hitting a white chick. A white guy stepped up to defend the girl. The result was a racial fight with about eight blacks and six whites participating. Hearing the disturbance from the kitchen, I moved out into the hallway leading to the large dining hall we were using for the dance. The major part of the fight was moving into the hall at the same time I was, so that is where I confronted the brawling mass.

I spoke firmly: "What seems to be the problem?" That was a rather foolish question. Obviously the problem was that they were fighting. At any rate, the response I received was startling. All became very quiet, the fighting ceased, and one black guy said, "It's cool, man, it's cool." It was really an exciting feeling to think that those few words stopped the whole thing. Just as I started feeling proud of myself, another black guy belted a white guy, and the whole thing started all over again. Fred Keene had been knocked down and was crawling on the floor looking for his glasses. Since he has one glass eye and the other is not too good, he was pretty helpless, so I got him to his feet. I tried to break up the fight, but there were so many fists flying that it had gotten out of my control.

Finally, the whites had had enough and began to back off. One, named Nick, a fiery-tempered New Yorker hooked on smack, had blood flowing from his head down the right side of his face. Another, Blue, who is partially crippled, was knocked down and kicked by a couple of guys; his head was bruised a little. The black dude who had tried to calm things down earlier finally succeeded in getting his friends to stop fighting, and they split. No one seemed to be hurt too seriously, though there were threats that next time it will be worse.

I think the blacks are from the ghettos around Oakland. They started coming regularly to the Avenue about nine months ago, Ray told me. To the already troubled Berkeley streets they brought the hip language characteristic of the ghetto, more drugs, the tendency to violence, and the seeming lack of reverence for life. The tough conditions of the ghetto have taught them the creed "Do unto others before they do it to you."

Middle-class whites (I include myself) for the most part do not know the laws of the ghetto. We have been relatively sheltered and spoiled, unable to understand life in the ghetto. Violence frightens us, and this fear, coupled with our incapacity and lack of desire to understand, is undoubtedly the major reason behind the migration of many Americans to the ranks of the far right.

Mainstream America has done its best to avoid confrontation with the ghetto. Migration of the "decent" population to suburbia has at least temporarily separated them from most contacts with ghetto people and their problems. On the one hand, I can really understand the plight of the suburbanites: Who wants to raise kids in a jungle where any day they might get assaulted; where survival is of the toughest, not the kindest; where stealing is for kicks; sex with any chick is groovy; persuasion is with fists, brass knuckles, and broken bottles? I have no trouble at all understanding how parents would not want their children to grow up in that kind of environment.

On the other hand, the problems of the ghetto grow fast. As suburbia grows, so grows the ghetto. Our cities have become battlegrounds where the fight is more serious than for better jobs and more pay; the fight is for survival. And I do not mean just physical survival. At stake are the physical, psychological, social, and spiritual lives of millions of human beings who are Americans.

These problems must be confronted. Not by more police who are often more like foreign invaders than protectors of the peace. And not by louder screams for law and order, nor by guns in the hands of a panic-stricken group of right-wing Americans. They must be confronted by suffering love. Blood may be shed, but the blood of suffering love contains power, a power superior to the power of atomic bombs.

Violence met with violence is the way of men. God enters the picture when men choose to go the way of God, the way of suffering love. Suffering love means being beaten and robbed by a couple of whites, blacks, or chicanos but not giving way to hatred or desire for revenge; it is turning the other cheek. It is giving love to people and spending time with them even when we don't want to, not because they deserve it, but because we realize they need us, and that the love we give and the Lord we share are many times the only chance they have.

Suffering love is having a daughter raped, or killed, in the ghetto, but, rather than calling for more "law and order," calling for more giving, more loving, laws which are more just, more money spent on education, housing, and health services.

Suffering love is being there, even when it hurts; it is seeing beauty in ugliness, seeing the face of Jesus Christ in every human being. It is being a friend to those who have no friends; it is showing love to those who know only hatred.

It is laying your life on the line with the willingness, if need be, to give it up for a friend. That is the law of suffering love; it is the life we are all called to live by the two simple words of Jesus: "Follow me." It is easier to write about than it is to live. Without the Spirit of God within us it is impossible.

We must learn to see the power in this love. Jesus overcame. He overcame the power of evil, and he overcame death.

19 · Twenty-Four and Free Again

July 20

I became 24 years old two days ago. The day also brought a significant change of direction in my life. Since arriving in Berkeley I have spent almost all my time with street people, seeking as best I could to love them, understand them, and help them. Although I have met some other Christians, my contacts with them have been for the most part coincidental and rare.

For a few days last week I was feeling particularly the effects of the lack of Christian fellowship. I have always considered this fellowship important and little did I know until recently just how important it really is.

The street culture was gradually pulling me into itself; and, although it was essential that I come to understand it on the basis of genuine involvement in it, it was also essential that I not conform to it in ways that would prove harmful to my development as a person and as a follower of Jesus Christ. Having adapted adequately to the situation, I was able to relate to the street people with self-assurance, and this has proved to be a prerequisite for talking to them about the value of the Christian faith. My failure was not an inability to communicate, but was rather that I adapted too well. My thoughts often were lustful; I laughed heartily at jokes more sick than humorous; and my language was becoming a little foul. I could feel my effectiveness as a "Christian presence" dwindling and, though I enjoyed a new popularity with many, I realized that my friendship in itself was inadequate to bring about lasting positive change in the lives of my friends.

The street culture had a greater hold on me than I realized and, try as I would, I found it just about impossible to keep myself clean in thoughts and words. A spiritual battle was taking place within me, and it was becoming a burden for me. I came to see that only the Power of God could free me from my burden, not the power of Clay Ford.

On the night of the sixteenth I brought the matter before God, genuinely sorry for my failures. I asked that he forgive me and then resigned myself to carry the burden as long as God thought necessary.

God never ceases to amaze me. Within two days I was free again, once more filled with his love and Spirit. It was undoubtedly the finest birthday present I have ever received. It happened when I went to a Christian folk-rock concert at Palo Alto with a few Christian friends I'd met earlier in the summer. On the way we stopped at a supermarket and loaded up on plums, oranges, sunflower seeds, and a big jug of apple cider to go with the sandwiches and cupcakes we already had. We arrived at Stanford University's outdoor amphitheater, where the concert was held, shortly after two o'clock. It was a beautiful day—not a cloud in sight—no fog or smog; just blue sky, warm, luscious sunshine, soft grass and pillows we brought with us in the bus. About 3,000 persons were there, the majority of whom were Christians. There is something extraordinarily beautiful, joyful, peaceful, fulfilling, and out-of-sight about three thousand Christians praising Christ together, singing about him, dancing in his joy and love in the warmth of the sun on a summer afternoon. I felt like I was floating on a cloud of love, bathing in gentle kisses of angels.

Four groups sang, including The Salt Company from the First Presbyterian Church in Hollywood and a group of soul-sisters from the Los Angeles Area. The last song of the festival, sung by all the groups, was "Oh, Happy Day." Nearly everyone in the audience sang along with them, standing, shouting, dancing in huge circles and in lines, keeping time with the beat of the music. Three thousand cheering, joyous, love-filled people praising their Lord—straights and hippies, young and old, blacks, browns, reds, and whites alike, clasping hands with their brothers and sisters in Christ.

After the music was over, a black dude spoke. I'm not sure of his name. This guy was tremendous! He spoke with *power*, man! Every sentence was followed by prolonged enthusiastic applause. Perhaps the excitement of everyone gave him a boost, but even so I have never heard such a powerful speaker. And he spoke in the language of the people.

The effect of that day on me is difficult to describe. My faith was restored in full, that which had been drained away was replenished. I became engulfed with joy and my greatest desire was to serve and share. "Because he cleaves to me in love, I will deliver him; I will protect him, because he knows my name"

(Ps. 91:14, RSV). "But the path of the righteous is like the light of dawn, which shines brighter and brighter until full day" (Prov. 4:18, RSV). "Praise ye the LORD. Praise the LORD, O my soul. While I live will I praise the LORD: I will sing praises unto my God while I have any being" (Ps. 146:1–2, AV).

20 · A Friend and Brother

July 21

On an afternoon two days ago as I was sitting up on the Cal campus I spotted a pretty blond with bright blue eyes walking toward me. It was Janice, a member of the Christian World Liberation Front, whom I had met not long ago. She mentioned that a college group from one of the Berkeley churches was having a free picnic at Tilden Park. Janice said she and her roommate were going and asked if I wanted to go. "Why not?" We saw Tony and Paul, two regulars at the coffee house, and asked if they wanted to come too. "Why not?" On my way to my room I saw Smith and asked if he wanted to come. "Why not?" When we got to the host church, which is one block from the Baptist Church, Satan, our kitchen volunteer and coffee house regular, was also there ready to go.

The picnic turned out to be a humorous situation. There were only six members of the church group but 12 of us guests. We had to pool our money into a common fund and go buy some food. I was chosen to be treasurer and before I knew it I had over nine dollars in my hands. People aren't tight when it comes to filling their own bellies. We got hot dogs, different kinds of chips and dips, salad, marshmallows, and drinks. Then we drove into the hills overlooking Berkeley to a park for the picnic.

Things were a little uneasy at first. The church people were straight for the most part and were apprehensive about fellowship with the street people, not knowing how to relate with them. The street people were uncomfortable around the straights and the CWLF kids, who have a reputation for being verbal about their Christian faith. Perhaps it was natural then that Smith, Tony, and Paul went over the hill by themselves for a little while to smoke a joint and size up the situation. And it was probably just as natural for those from the church group to sit off by themselves a little distance from the rest of us. I sat down with this group for a while, talking in particular with a young woman who turned out to be a nurse. I sensed in her a deep commitment to her work, which is helping those in physical need. While I was talking with her I noticed Smith sitting by himself on a bank. He was not eating anything, so I went over and sat beside him to see what was wrong. This decision turned out to be the best thing that happened, and indeed one of the real highlights of the summer thus far.

Smith was sitting on the grass drilling a hole with a long, crooked stick. He looked up at me briefly as I sat down beside him and then looked back down at the hole he was drilling. He was in a quiet, thoughtful mood and seemed a little sad. I asked him what was the matter.

"Nothing."

"Why aren't you eating?"

"Not hungry."

"Oh."

I paused for a moment, wondering if the problem was that he did not like the people at the picnic, or if there was some other reason. It suddenly dawned on me that God was working on him, that he was hungry—not for food but for the Bread of Life —and thirsty—not for soda pop but for the Living Water. I had talked with him of Christ often before, and he knew what it was all about. I sat wondering how best to bring up the subject now.

I cannot remember exactly what I said. I happened to have a Four Laws booklet in my hip pocket and I gave it to him to read. He opened it and read very intensely all the way through. I asked him if he understood what he had to do if he wanted to be a Christian. He said he did. I wanted to make sure. So many times people commit themselves to Christ without really understanding what they are doing, only later to feel they were tricked into it, that someone had "sugarcoated" Christianity for them.

Smith began drilling his hole again. Then he pulled something out of his pocket and looked at it for a moment. It was a tab of acid. I stopped talking and looked at it too, wondering if he were going to drop it into his mouth. We looked at that tab together for about ten seconds. It seemed like ten minutes. Then without saying a word, he tossed the tab of acid right into the middle of the hole he had drilled. He crushed it with his stick and covered it up with dirt. For a full fifteen seconds we were both silent. It was a silence pregnant with meaning. Smith became a Christian.

This was a powerful moment for me. I had grown to love Smith in spite of his Bad Conduct Discharge, his drug abuse, foul language, and violent nature. We were friends and now we were brothers. For this I praise God!

Soon all of us gathered on the bank and began to sing songs, some Christian, some not. The apprehension existing before had melted away as ice when it touches fire. The fellowship became relaxed and joyful. The last song we sang before leaving was "How Great Thou Art." My heart was bursting with awe and love for this Great One; it was all I could do to hold back the tears. Smith is my brother; but, what is more important, he is a child of God.

21 · Pentecost

July 23

Yesterday I went up to the hills with Smith, Alabama, a girl named Martie, and Mona, who is from Chile. We went to pick blackberries but unfortunately we found less than a dozen. On the way back we were passing through a residential area and Alabama asked me to stop the car. He wanted to knock on someone's door and bum a cigarette. We thought he was kidding, but I decided to stop to see if he would really do it. When he got out we zipped down the road and turned a corner, pretending to leave him. We turned around and came back about 30 seconds later, but he had disappeared.

We looked all around for him, got out of the car and yelled his name. No answer. We began to worry that something had happened to him. Martie and I checked the houses to see if anyone had knocked on the doors. No one had seen Alabama. We were a little worried but figured he had probably gotten a ride with someone else and was playing a trick on us.

When we got back to the church, we saw him. Grinning broadly, he told us how he ran around the corner when we dropped him off and caught a ride. He went on to say that he did something very important while he was sitting there waiting for another ride. We asked him to go on.

He smiled and then said, "I asked Jesus into my life."

I almost fell over: "You're kidding!"

"Nope. I really did it."

He really had.

Alabama and Smith both Christians! I have a taste of what the first Christians must have felt when God poured out his Spirit upon them on the Day of Pentecost; those Christians were so exuberant and overwhelmed by the love of God which changed their lives that others accused them of being drunk. I feel "intoxicated" with God's love. It is the power of his love that has drawn Smith and Alabama to himself; and it is the power of his love that will transform their lives as they yield more completely to him and seek to be like him.

22 · A Bolder Witness

July 29

My life-changing experiences of the last few weeks have made me a bolder witness to Jesus Christ. The changing began on my birthday when I was strengthened in faith and filled with God's Spirit. I was revitalized again when Smith and Alabama became Christians, and also when some of the other street people I know accepted Christ through the ministry of the CWLF. My deeper relationship with God has also affected my relationship with the world and with my neighbor, causing a question to turn over and over in my mind. In the ever-increasing polarization between Establishment and anti-Establishment, where do I, Clay Ford, a Christian and student for the ministry, fit in? My faith in God goes beyond the issues of everyday politics, but my duty to serve him calls me to take a stand on these issues.

Earlier in the summer I talked with pseudo-boldness about the implications of being a Christian in America. I lambasted the Establishment on the one hand and the dissidents and revolutionaries on the other. And by not taking either side I thought that I could see things clearly and objectively. But I was deceiving myself. While pointing out the hypocrisy all around me, I was subtly allowing myself to feel that I was free of hypocrisy. I was paving my way to a smug, noncommittal type of self-righteousness.

I realize now that I was part of the Establishment all along, that I did not really identify with the poor, but with the rich; not with the oppressed, but with the oppressor. My ideas were right, for the most part, but the rest of me lagged behind. Perhaps this is the way the human psyche works. The mind trips across something and perceives it to be the truth. But belief in the truth is not enough; one must conform to the truth and incorporate it into his very being. This is what happened to me in the last week. The truth I perceived has become a part of me. I am no longer a fence-sitter. I am no longer a tacit supporter of the Establishment. I must align myself against it.

For a long time I was not sure whether I should take a stand on political and social questions. Many Christians I love and respect think that Christianity is a purely spiritual matter. They believe that the Christian's only mission is evangelism—saving souls. But now I see that if Christ is truly my Lord, then he is Lord of all my life, not just of my spiritual capacities. Am I to tell him that I don't think he can handle any part of me besides the spiritual? It is clear to me that my Christian faith has a great deal to say about the economic and political parts of life.

Working in the Berkeley street culture and reading books such as *Why We Can't Wait*, *Black Rage*, and *Soul on Ice* have enabled me to view conditions in America from a new perspective. I see for the first time the really deep evils of racism. I see that materialism is as much a part of America as the stars and stripes and popcorn at the movies. I understand how in our insatiable desire for material goods we are polluting our air and fields.

At first these facts scared me. I grew up in a middle-class

home, went to a middle-class private college, and have associated for most of my life with people of a similar background. When I came to Berkeley I identified with the status quo in America. It took me awhile, once I perceived the truth, to make it a part of my life because I knew that change would perhaps jeopardize my future and alienate me from those who have been my friends.

23 · Blind Revolutionaries

July 30

I've been spending time with some Mao-type revolutionaries, reading their stuff and trading ideas with them. A couple of things about them bug me. They are quick to point out the ills of capitalism in America—and I see what they see. They are quick to point out the oppression of certain groups in this country—and I see that too. But they don't seem to notice the oppression of persons in Russia or China who don't dig the government. They blind themselves to the truth if it doesn't substantiate what they want to see.

Another thing that disturbs me is that the serious revolutionaries whom I have met here are, with few exceptions, driven by intense hatred. They have cell meetings as Christians have Bible studies, and to motivate their supporters they show their films of the "People's Park" disturbances, the San Francisco State University strike, and incidents of police brutality. But, unlike Christian groups who psych their people to love in response to God's love through Jesus Christ, violent revolutionaries psych themselves to hate and to destroy. To the extent that violent revolutionaries are driven by hate, they are the incarnation of evil.

God has taught us through Christ that power resides in suffering love—power that transforms sickness into health and death into life. Gandhi and Martin Luther King teach us the same thing—that power lies in nonviolent resistance when the cause is right and when there is love rather than animosity toward the enemy. Gandhi believed that nonviolent acts can have more power than all the devices of violence known to man. Nonviolent acts are one of man's ways of inviting God into human history, of plugging into the Source of love and justice and allowing him to work through us in the world.

24 · Blue

July 31

A revolutionary chick who comes to the church for meals really fascinates me. I call her Blue because of her ocean-blue eyes. She is 19, tall, and has long brownish-reddish blond hair. Quiet but confident and able to handle herself, Blue is clean-looking even in her usual attire of blue jeans, shirt, and baggy sweater. Smoking pot appeals to her, but she doesn't mess with anything else.

Blue has a mysterious way about her that keeps guys from bothering her. On one occasion a guy came up to her, his hands and facial expression making clear his intentions; he asked as he was approaching, "I wonder if Blue knows how to take care of herself . . . ha, ha . . ." She didn't move an inch but looked him square in the eye and said firmly, "You're . . . right I do." He stopped dead in his tracks, blushed from humiliation, turned around and walked away. Some of the guys, resenting her brush-off of their amorous attempts, have spread rumors that she is a lesbian. I'm sure after talking with her about it that the rumors are not true. She gets along with both guys and girls but none of her relationships are physical, which is unusual in the street culture.

Blue grew up in a relatively poor family in California. Her parents are separated but she was close to both of them until high school when she became radicalized. Her mother began working hard to make a career for herself in a man's world, and eventually she succeeded in the field of data processing. She moved from her poor home into a well-to-do suburban residential area, purchasing a large, expensive home. Blue is glad her mother has made it on her own in a world stacked against women who want a career; however, her mother feels that because she has worked hard and made it through her own efforts, she is entitled to the luxuries of the high life she was without for so long. Since Blue is a committed revolutionary, I wonder what her feelings toward her mother will be when the fighting starts.

Blue goes to the cell meetings of the local revolutionary groups. She takes in their films, reads their propaganda, and sides with the extreme left on all the issues. I asked her once what caused her to become a revolutionary, but the only answer she would give is, "I tried real hard." She doesn't relish violence, indeed she is a gentle and sensitive person, but she says that when the fighting starts she'll do her part. She uses obscene language as does the rest of the Berkeley street community. But the words do not fit her.

Blue likes to keep busy. A frequent face at the church, she bakes bread in the kitchen. She was making bread one day when Smith, Alabama, and I were there. Rolling the dough in a big ball and throwing it down hard on the board looked fun so Smith, Alabama, and I asked if we could help. We took turns throwing the dough down as hard as we could. It became a contest to see who could throw it down the hardest. We got tired of waiting our turn so we declared an all-out war on that dough and beat it with our fists, yelling without mercy. Poor Blue. At first she just looked sadly at her creation taking such a beating, but then she too joined in. The bread came out of the oven really delicious, even though it had fallen on the dirty floor a few times!

Blue sews some, too. She was sitting in the runaway center once sewing a monogram on a shirt. I kidded her, "You sure have been getting domesticated lately, Blue. What's going on?" She blushed, particularly embarrassed because she sympathizes with the Women's Liberation Movement, whose members often reject roles such as sewing and cooking which are traditionally associated with womanhood in America. Although she denies it strongly, I think she has longings to be a wife and mother some day.

A karate class for girls meets during the day in the coffee house room of the church. Over 50 fighting females are learning that art of self-defense. Blue is one of them. Most of the girls are affiliated with Women's Liberation. The class instructor is male and, as it turns out, the only male allowed in the room at the time the class meets. A couple of guys opened the door the other day and walked in; in less than two seconds they were back out the door. This little episode aroused my curiosity. Why had the two guys left in such a hurry? Maybe they had handled the situation wrong.

I began toying with the idea of trying my own luck, and felt like a little boy plotting to sneak into the kitchen and pilfer a few cookies. The more I thought about it, the more curious I became. It wasn't that I wanted to watch them learn karate so much as it was that I wanted to see if they'd let me get away with watching them. I realized that the whole thing was silly, but decided to go ahead with it anyway.

I thought that, since I work at the coffee house, maybe they wouldn't hassle me at all, especially if I walked in nonchalantly as though I knew what I was doing. I paced the floor 20 or 30 times outside the door making sure no one was around and also trying to get up my courage for the daring mission. Finally I felt ready. I wiped the sweat off my hands, swung the door wide open, and walked in as nonchalantly as I could. Man, I mean I was *super*-nonchalant. But no sooner had I taken two steps inside when what seemed like thousands of girls ran angrily toward me demanding that I leave. I looked briefly at them as if to say, "You must be making some mistake; I work here." They responded with a look that said, "No, dude—you're the one making a big mistake if you don't split—like Now!" I smiled sickly and, losing my cool, made a bumbling retreat out the door. I'm sure if I'd stayed, I would have landed in the hospital.

I can understand why these girls have so much hostility toward men. Many of them have been sexually and economically exploited by the male species of Berkeleyites. Blue shares their hostilities, but in her case it's more a mood she gets into once in a while than a general attitude.

One day last week Blue and I went to Big Sur. We hiked for a while and then swam in the Pacific at Carmel Beach. I took a book on Christianity and Communism, and we talked about it for awhile. Blue seems to have a deep-seated resistance to accepting Christianity, probably because of what it would cost her in peer acceptance.

25 · Santa Rita Prison

August 5

Things aren't the same at the coffee house with Cheyenne gone. Smith and I went to see him at Santa Rita two weeks ago.

We waited in line for over half an hour before we got through the prison gates, only to discover we had another half-hour wait in the visitors' line. We looked through the wire for Cheyenne but he was nowhere to be seen. We asked a few inmates but they either didn't know him or didn't know where he was. Then we got an officer to look for him. As it turned out, Cheyenne had figured on us coming the week before so he had sat waiting and nobody showed up. When we came the following week, he didn't expect us and he didn't come out for visitation. We left him a message by way of one of his prison friends.

Our next word from Cheyenne was a note a few days ago that really boosted our morale. It was addressed to Smith and me and was delivered personally by one of his friends who had just been released. The note said that he was sorry he hadn't gotten to see us when we came and that he wanted us to come again. Then he wrote, "Tell Clay his prayers are being answered; I'm telling everyone here about God." That thrilled my heart. Cheynne is carrying on a ministry right there in prison. Perhaps this experience is proving to Cheyenne that "all things work together for good to them that love God, to them who are called according to his purpose" (Rom. 8:28, AV). I have no idea when Cheyenne will get out. Soon, I hope. But I no longer feel so bad about his being in prison; he's doing good work for the Lord and is apparently in good spirits.

26 · Reluctant to Believe

August 6

I wrote earlier about a friend named Terry who is deep in the transcendental meditation movement. He's been spending a lot of time with me lately; he's also been spending time with some of the CWLF people. I believe he is with Christians more than with anyone else, yet he simply turns off and snarls whenever one of his Christian friends starts talking about Jesus Christ. He seems to be torn inside. He sees qualities that he likes in Christians, or he wouldn't seek our company. On the other hand, something inside him ties him into knots when Jesus is the topic of conversation. He's been going through a lot of anguish because of his inner conflicts.

I talked to him one day about his religious background. He said he grew up in the Catholic Church. When he was a young boy, he explained, "I prayed to God and he was real." But since that time he has drifted away and now realizes that the faith he once had was childish. I told him that it is common for the faith of a child to be childish, and that, should he become a sincere Christian now, he could expect a much deeper, more mature, and more fulfilling faith.

On another occasion with Terry I directed the conversation to Christian sex morality. It, I believe, is the point of his most bitter criticism against the Christian faith. He wants his own way on this.

"Sex can be beautiful," he said.

"No kidding," I responded. "The Bible makes that pretty clear." I went on to explain how God had made us male and female and had given us sexual capacities and how he wants us to enjoy them. But that he wants us to enjoy them within the framework of a loving, lasting, faithful, and responsible relationship. I explained that the Christian view maintains that sex is beautiful, that it is the deepest unity possible between a man and a woman because it involves all of each partner's body, mind, and spirit. And I explained that God gave us this capacity, both for our enjoyment and for the propagation of the race, but also—and very importantly—as an instrument through which two persons might truly become one, both physically and spiritually. The sex act is very deep and has lasting consequences, I told him, whether the persons involved are aware of it or not, or whether they want it that way or not.

He accused me of talking from my head and not from personal experience. I told him about my life before I met Jesus Christ, how I had been a reckless playboy. And I told him I still had spiritual and emotional scars left from the deep wounds of irresponsible sexual relationships.

Terry was silent for awhile. Then he spoke: "What's true for you isn't necessarily true for me." I'm sure he knew I was sincere and was speaking from my heart. But he just did not want to believe what I was saying. He fought back against the wave of conviction that had briefly come over him, and he rationalized his way so that he could feel comfortable. I love Terry. It hurts me that he won't give Jesus a chance in his life.

27 · Satanists

August 10

The worshipers of Satan are one of the groups competing for attention in Berkeley. The Satanists are members, I believe, of the Church of Satan across the bay in San Francisco. They meet regularly in small groups called "covens" for the purpose of aligning themselves with occult powers which they use to accomplish their evil desires. One of a coven's evil designs is to put a hex or curse on a particular person; this, the Satanists claim, has caused blindness and even death. A less evil practice of the Satanists is to call upon the powers of the occult for money or a certain job.

The Satanists value all the characteristics abominable to Christians, namely, lust, greed, pride, hatred, and fornication.

They despise Christian values like love, humility, selflessness, purity, and honesty. In a book which they call their "bible" they have adapted the Christian Bible, distorting it so that their values are good and God's values are not. The Satanists believe that they are plugged into a source of power. Satanism is spreading along with a proliferation of the witch cults. But, as its name indicates, Satanism is rooted in evil.

Many people in Berkeley and elsewhere are toying with Satanism, witchcraft, ouija boards, seances, and spirit-communication. When they discover it works, they become more involved in it. That it works, there is little doubt; that it is evil is even less doubtful. Christians are aware of the spiritual dimension of life, for through it they have become channels of God's love and God's power. Satanists and the growing numbers practicing witchcraft of various kinds are also discovering the spiritual dimension of life. However, they are aligning themselves with forces that are in opposition to God and his purpose. As they get further into Satan-worship, they become channels of Satan's powers much like Christians become channels of God's powers. I see a great spiritual warfare in the making. I am deeply concerned for those who wander innocently into these things and become swallowed up in them. They are playing with fire, and fire destroys.

The Satanists in Berkeley behave much the way in relation to Christians as one would expect Satan to behave toward God. Satan is the deceiver, the would-be sabateur of all God's plans and purposes. Likewise, the Satanists sabotage the efforts of Christian evangelists in Berkeley. The apparent leader of the Satanists in Berkeley is Mal. He wears shiny black leather pants, a black cape, has long black hair and cold dark eyes with a tinge of red in them. That sounds almost like a figure out of a fairy tale, but it is an accurate description. He is muscular, handsome in a rugged sort of way, plays a guitar, and sings in a very deep voice. His right-arm companion is named Roller, who is very big with bushy hair; he seems never to have any color in his face, but is always pale.

On one occasion Hubert, the most popular evangelist in Berkeley, was preaching and Mal came up and started harassing him. Hubert is sharp and able to take care of himself verbally; he usually outwits Mal in their verbal volleys but this time Mal was so gross that Hubert left. As Hubert was preaching, Mal yelled "Fornication—Yea-a-a!" He repeated it every few seconds, very loudly. Hubert was standing on a little platform he carries around with him, and Mal started dancing around the platform yelling "Fornication." Hubert controlled the situation for awhile and quieted the laughter of the crowd. But then Mal started dancing with a girl member of the Satanist cult, and they both yelled "Fornication!" and began simulating the sex act. It was so repulsive, I thought I'd vomit. The expressions on the faces of Mal and the girl were so evil; never before have I seen eyes like theirs, so sinister and perverted. This incident is an indication of the purpose of the Satanists and the lengths to which they go to accomplish that purpose.

Yesterday afternoon I had a brief encounter with Mal and Roller. A young preacher named David was giving away pocket-sized New Testaments at Sproul Plaza to those who promised to read them. David is sponsored by a Bible society; his primary job is to travel around the country giving away Bibles. He's been in Berkeley for several days now. Mal and Roller went up to him and pretended they wanted a Bible; they got one and then walked a few feet away, got out a book of matches, and set fire to the Bible. Mal and Roller laughed gleefully as it burned. I watched David. His eyes were sorrowful as he saw the precious words of his Lord go up in smoke. He looked at Mal and Roller as though he couldn't believe they were real. This was probably his first encounter with Satanists.

David kept passing out his Bibles and soon a crowd of about 25 persons gathered around him. Someone asked him a question, and, as he responded, Mal moved next to him and began yelling "Hail, Satan!" into his ear. David stammered a little, uncertain of how to handle the situation. Every time he opened his mouth, Mal would yell "Hail, Satan!" One guy there, who was apparently a friend of Mal's, had been asking serious questions before Mal began his offensive attack. When Mal started, his friend forgot his questions and joined Mal in harassing David, though he didn't seem to have his heart in it as much as Mal did.

Mal stepped away for some reason, and I took the opportunity to move into the space that he had occupied beside David. I said a quick prayer as I saw Mal returning, asking God to be with me and somehow to use me for good in this situation. Mal made his way through the crowd. He looked a little disgusted as he saw his friend once more engaged in a serious conversation with this Christian who was distributing Bibles. He made his way right by me and said, "Excuse me," as he tried to shove me to one side. I stood my ground and said, "I'm standing here." He yelled in a sarcastic tone "Oh *you're* standing here. Well, *excuse me.*" He then stepped away—I hoped to stay—but within one minute he returned with Roller. One got on each side of me and began shoving me away.

At that moment something powerful happened; it was God's answer to my prayer. A black dude who was in the crowd apparently had been watching my encounter with Mal. He put his hand on Roller's shoulder and said, "Hey, cool it, man; he's standing there." Mal and Roller stood stunned for a second. Then Mal said, "He's the one that tried to . . ." Before Mal could finish, this black guy interrupted, "Quit jiving, man; I saw what happened."

Apparently Mal had never been confronted like this before. He and Roller looked at each other, then at me. Both of them apologized and shook my hand. Then Mal saw his friend still engaged in a serious conversation with David. Mal asked, "Are you starting to believe that stuff?" His friend retorted. "Don't bug me, man." Mal and Roller walked away powerless and defeated. When I looked at Mal, his head hanging low in defeat, he was the picture of a whining dog, running away with its tail between its legs. That's exactly how Satan flees from the power of Jesus Christ.

Satan is a reality, a live, spiritual force. His purpose is to distort, pervert, deceive, and destroy all that is good, fulfilling, and true—in other words, all that is of God. He is second in power only to God and his Son, Jesus Christ. The origin of Satan I am uncertain about; but one look into the eyes of Mal is more than enough evidence that he exists. As the person of Christ exudes from Spirit-filled Christians, so does the person of Satan exude from Mal.

Mal is a powerful individual. He has quite an influence here because of his good looks and his ability to sing and to play the guitar. He is so engulfed by Satan that to become a Christian would require a complete reorientation of his life. Yet I know of a couple former Satanists who have become Christians.

28 · Barrington Hall, Tim, and Johnny

August 12

Barrington Hall, a large building about a half-block from the church, is home for some of the street people. Formerly a U.C. dormitory, it is now privately owned, and rooms are rented for about $30 a month. Some of the street people gather enough money to pay the rent by panhandling, which is asking for spare change from passersby on the sidewalk. Others deal in drugs or "rip off" (steal) books, clothes, etc., and sell them. Still others receive unemployment or welfare payments for psychological difficulties. A number of unwed pregnant teenage girls who receive money from the government live at Barrington Hall. And others who live there receive money from their parents who may be well-to-do prominent citizens somewhere back East.

The majority of street people, however, don't have rooms of their own. They sleep on the floors of those who have rooms, on the rooftops of apartment houses and office buildings, inside churches they can break into, in vacant lots behind big clumps of grass, or in the hills overlooking Berkeley—anywhere they can find where they won't be hassled by the police. The only meal many, if not most, of them get every day is the meal we serve at the church, where from 300 to 500 eat six days a week.

Tim is one of the hundreds who have been involved in our food program at the church. Twenty-two years old, he is slightly crippled from polio. Although each street person is unique and has his own story, Tim is fairly representative of a large percentage of those in Berkeley in that he is a misfit. He can't make it in school nor can he find his niche in the job world. He doesn't know where his family is and bitterly claims he doesn't care either. What he finds in Berkeley is a place where people like him, who can't seem to find their place in life, can escape at least one kind of emotional anguish. Outside the street culture they are made to feel worthless or freakish, because they can't make good grades, or because their physical or psychological difficulties make them undesirable or unable to produce at the clip expected of them. They are made to feel like tools, as means to an end, rather than as ends in themselves. In the straight world their value as persons is more often seen in terms of dollars and cents rather than in terms of the sacredness of human life created by God.

Some of these misfits are serious radicals and have committed their all to the destruction of America. Others, like Tim, are radical only because they thirst for acceptance, love, and attention; in Berkeley they can get attention and sometimes acceptance by being verbally radical. At last they can attain that precious awareness that they are part of something big and important: the Revolution. The misfits often become more radical once they begin to project their own personal failure and frustrations onto the Establishment.

On one occasion Tim angrily described to me the People's Park episode of a few years ago. "People's Park" was the name given to a plot of land just east of Telegraph Avenue. Owned by the University of California, it lay idle for a period of time after old buildings had been torn down. The street culture, many Berkeley students, and even some straight adult citizens of the Berkeley community began using the land as a park. They planted flowers and trees, played ball, threw frisbees, and had picnics. Suddenly the U.C. regents announced that the land was the property of the university, that they needed it for a parking lot and recreation field, and that "the people" would have to clear out. The people refused. Then a wire fence was constructed around the park and demonstrating students and street people tore it down. Riots broke out and one person was killed and many others injured. At stake was the whole issue of private property rights. Is it fair for a small minority of men with money and political power to make decisions regarding what will be done with land when those decisions affect the lives of the great majority who have no voice in the decision-making process? Or, shouldn't the people, the citizens of the Berkeley community, have some voice in the matter? A lot of blood was shed over this issue.

Tim explained to me his role in the People's Park incidents: "My fiancée and I were watching the riots when suddenly we saw a bunch of army tanks coming up the street. We could hardly believe our eyes."

"Army tanks?" I asked. "I don't remember reading about any tanks in the paper."

"Do you think they'd put that in the paper?" he asked.

I answered, "Sure, but even if the regular press didn't, I'm sure the underground press wouldn't have failed to."

He went on with his story, his eyes aglow with excitement, apparently disregarding my rebuttal of his story about the tanks. He seemed in a trance as he went on: "Those tanks came up the street and opened fire on us."

"Sure," I said sarcastically. He ignored me.

"A bullet struck my fiancée in the temple of her head, and she died instantly. Weeping bitterly I ran to get a bomb I had hidden for emergencies. I ran after the tanks and spotted the one that had killed her. It turned on me and came directly toward me. I dived on the ground. It just missed me. I jumped up, threw the bomb under it, and ran for my life. That thing exploded into thousands of pieces. What a sight!"

"Wow!" I exclaimed. "That's really something." His eyes sparkled. He apparently thought he had convinced me he was telling the truth. Then I asked him, "Do you really expect me to believe that? What a bunch of garbage!" He didn't speak to me for two days.

More recently, however, I have become one of Tim's heroes. He has started praising me for various things almost every time he sees me. It started one day when he and I were sitting in the runaway center in the basement of the church. The room was filled with about 20 street people just passing the time, rapping. On that occasion, the usual tension of the street culture melted. We started laughing and enjoying one another's fellowship. One fun thing we decided was that when the next person entered the room we would all get up at once and walk out. A guy walked in, and without saying a word, we all got up and started walking out. His expression was so stunned, a couple of us just couldn't hold back any longer. We laughed until tears came rolling down our cheeks. We explained to the guy what we were doing, and he laughed with us. Then we did it several more times, and each time it seemed funnier. There was a good feeling in that room, a warmth and acceptance very uncharacteristic of the street culture.

Later Tim came up to me and told me he knew that I was

responsible for that feeling in the room, that he knew I had something, and that he felt God through me and knew he was with me. Since that time he has praised me time and again, saying that I have beautiful vibes and that I have taught a lot of people that you don't have to treat other people lousy, that it's better to love. Naturally, this made me feel good because it's my greatest purpose to be a vessel of God's love, God's vibes. But after his wild tale about the tanks, I don't know how seriously to take anything Tim says.

Tim passes himself off as a palm reader sometimes. He's pretty good at it too. He amazes people with his ability to describe personality traits, problems, and yearnings. Actually, he is very sensitive and perceptive in some intuitive ways. I got him to admit to me one day that his palm reading is a hoax. He said he depends on his natural ability to feel with the person and to pick up visual cues. He pokes around in a particular area and reads the person's response, which enables him to go a step farther. He said he depends a good deal upon luck, too.

I've grown to love Tim. He is usually kind and gentle, though he's been known to lose his head on occasion. The street culture environment is not the best for him. But he, like so many other street people, really has no place else to go. He will not go straight, because he would not be accepted as a worthwhile human being within the rigid Pharisaic value-structure of straight society. A loving community of Christians is his best hope.

Probably the most emotionally disturbed individual I have met this summer is Johnny, from New York City. He spends a good part of his time sharpening a barber's razor and glaring at anyone who tries to calm him down or keep him from stealing food or equipment from the church kitchen. I had to get after him once for trying to steal a bag of sugar. Since that time he glares threateningly and sharpens his barber's razor almost every time he sees me. It's frightening in a way, especially since he is probably psychologically messed up enough to use that razor with the slightest provocation. Paul, in I Thessalonians, tells us to pray without ceasing. Situations like this one make that almost possible.

29 · It's Big Time Being a Scorpio

August 15

The astrology scene attracts the street people in Berkeley. Though they ask each other what sign they are, Scorpio, Capricorn, Leo, etc., most of them don't have any idea what the signs mean. When I'm asked, I always tell the questioner to guess. So far only one has guessed it right—Cancer, or Moon Children. Somebody brought in a big book on astrology not long ago, and hours were spent by various people figuring out clues to their personalities and to what the future might have in store for them. Sam seemed to be the only one who understood how to use the book, so he spent the most time with it. You had to trace down numbers and codes; it was a very complicated system. I read the statements corresponding to my numbers. Everything I read seemed to conflict with everything else I read.

Very few of those who pursue astrology take it seriously; it's just something different to do. It points to a need deeper than the need to know what sign one is. When a person asks another what sign he is, the question underneath the words is "I want to relate to you. I want to be loved and accepted by you. Will you respond?" It's a way of reaching out for meaningful relationships. Astrology gives a person at least some kind of identity. Lots of street people have no self-identity. They don't have jobs; they aren't students; and they don't belong to organizations with which they can identify. Astrological signs provide them an opportunity to identify themselves with a group of people. I've heard a guy whose sign is Scorpio say with great pride and a gleam in his eye, "I'm a Scorpio," like, man, he's big time, being a Scorpio. He couldn't say, "I'm a doctor," or a janitor or a salesman or a student or a serious revolutionary. Nor would he want to say, "I'm a street person," or "I take drugs," because there is nothing unusual about that in the street culture. But "I'm a Scorpio," that's something else again. It's amazing when two or three Scorpios or other signs get together. They can be perfect strangers and act like long-lost brothers.

I've learned to play along with the astrology game most of the time, realizing that it's an attempt to build relationships. A person is complimented when someone asks what his or her sign is. It's the same as saying, "I think you're a neat person. I want to relate to you."

The street culture has a style of language that fits its life-style. One of the words that is widely used is "vibes." Vibes are personality vibrations, the nonverbal, nonvisible dimension of interpersonal relationships. They are the spiritual dimension of communication between persons. I think it's a great word. When a person is said to have "good vibes," it means that his personality radiates a comfortable, accepting atmosphere. "Bad vibes" mean that the personality radiates anxiety, hostility, and manipulation. A person with bad vibes may want to love a particular person, may even believe that he does and say "I love you." But if he has bad vibes, the words don't fool anybody except perhaps the one who says them. Vibes present a person, including his intent, as he is. Words may or may not do that. Young children are tremendous vibe-readers; words don't fool them at all.

Another commonplace term in the coffee house is "together." A together person is someone who is mentally stable and knows what is happening. Ordinarily he would be thought of as having good vibes, but not necessarily. A person who is not together is someone whose mind is not stable, one who can't cope with situations effectively. But a "together" person in the street culture might be considered a terribly "untogether" person elsewhere.

30 · One Who's on Top

August 17

A girl named Peggy bakes bread in the church kitchen and sells it. She uses some of the money for herself, but most of it she gives to a young unwed mother so she can pay her rent. Peggy's most noticeable physical characteristic is a little gold ring that she wears through one of her nostrils. I asked her one day why she wore the ring, and she answered, "I don't know." Usually warm and friendly, occasionally she gets angry at people who steal her bread or try to talk her into giving them some without paying. She has a little dog that follows her around. Her dog has a real problem with nerves; he's always shaking, and he looks cautiously at anyone who comes near him.

Peggy used to live in the back of a pickup truck she owns that contains a homemade camper. But one night not long ago someone broke in and raped her. Now she's living in the Berkeley Inn, a shabby hotel on Telegraph Avenue.

She fasts, going without food for days at a time. She says it's good for you, if you drink fruit juices while fasting. One time she decided to go for 20 days but only made it to eight. The eighth day was her birthday, and a friend of hers convinced her to eat on her birthday. Peggy has inspired me to try fasting. I have found it to be beneficial, both mentally and spiritually.

I find myself really liking Peggy. She has a lot of drive and willpower and is one of the few street people who seems to enjoy life and to be on top of things. Yet living here over a long period of time may cause her to succumb gradually to the values and habits of those around her.

31 · A Dead-End Trip

August 18

When I leave Berkeley, it will be almost like stepping out of life back into a playworld of hopscotch and ring-around-the-roses. Perhaps that is a little exaggerated, but life is so intense here that, once accustomed to it, life elsewhere may be a real drag. The needs are more serious here; the problems more urgent.

Life in Berkeley is hard; it is *very* hard. It takes more energy just to exist here than it does any place I have ever been. Though this is true primarily of the campus and street cultures of Berkeley, the intensity and difficulty of life cannot be limited to them, but extend beyond them to include the straight community. Police officers, city officials, clergymen, merchants, professors, and mothers—they all share the intensity and excitement of living here whether they want to or not. Perhaps it is this intensity that makes Berkeley a hard place to leave, and, after one leaves, seems to draw him back.

People in Berkeley are very much aware of things. Just to wander around the campus of Cal is an education, for a person can learn about everything from the latest police bust on one of "the people" to the most recent political developments in South America, Africa, and Asia. He can learn the progress of the political trials in the nation, the amount of money the United States has spent to kill every Vietcong, the latest news of the Mid-East situation, and the superiority of Peking's communism over Moscow's brand. He can become knowledgeable of Marxist, capitalist, and socialist ideologies; and he can come to understand the polarization of the "haves" and the "have-nots" which will soon overtake in significance the polarization of the Communist and free worlds. He can select from a smorgasbord of religions and learn, not from books, but from the evangelists of each religion; he can find out about Christianity, Satanism, Christian Science, Islam, forms of Hinduism, Buddhism, scientology, the Unified Family, and Meher Baba. Living in Berkeley gives one the sensation that he is on top of everything that is happening in the world.

I am writing this while sitting on the steps of Sproul Hall. A group of bongo drummers is pounding out rhythms about a hundred feet to my left, with a large crowd gathered around them, apparently mesmerized by the beat. Dogs barking, frizbees floating, people walking by, a baby crying. It is really a gorgeous day—solid blue sky, warm sunshine, a nice breeze.

The scene is relaxing, for the most part. Berkeley, however, is never completely relaxing, for there is always potential for hostilities, violence, and the unexpected. Sitting here, blocking out the overall context of life in Berkeley, it is possible to be relaxed and refreshed by the sunshine. But, to sit here and be aware of the overall context, it is difficult to be completely at ease. For I know that Berkeley is a sanctuary for those unacceptable anywhere else—the ex-cons, those mentally sick, those who hate, those looking for a way to get their kicks at the expense of other people. You can sit in Berkeley at just about any time and know that somewhere in this area a girl is in danger of being raped, a guy is selling acid or smack to a 14-year-old kid, some guy is considering taking his own life, and another girl may have lost her mind forever on a bum trip. In order to be relaxed, completely relaxed, a person would have to stop caring about human life, his own as well as that of other people.

For some in Berkeley life means nothing; they really do not care any more, or perhaps they never did. Many are ready to die for the Revolution against the world Establishment or against the Berkeley Police, not so much because they want to fight for the right, but simply because they are ready to die. Life holds no more surprises for them; they have taken their trips, freaked out on everything there is; they have misused sex until the sex act holds no meaning, contains no beauty, and has no purpose other than temporarily to alleviate a drive. The riots, the trips, the light sex, hassling and being hassled by the cops, ripping things off—it all becomes a drag, and nothing else is left to try. Sooner or later the self-defeating life-style of the Berkeley street person catches up with him. Deep down inside, he knows it's a bummer, a dead-end trip.

People need to feel their lives count for something. Jesus Christ meets this need as no other person or thing is able. Jesus Christ is alive; his love is strong and deep and real; his love is power that transforms human life. Serving him is life's highest privilege and greatest joy. Being filled with his Spirit is abundant life, life in all its fullness. In fellowship with Jesus, life becomes an exciting adventure. It is a costly adventure. It costs us our lives yielded in love and obedience to him. But for the first time we discover what life really is. We find ourselves. We are washed clean, able to respect ourselves and love our brothers and sisters. Our lives count for something.

32 · Berkeley's Kaleidoscope of Salvation

August 20

All summer I've sought to understand what creates a Berkeley. Why is there a street culture? What's behind this counter-culture movement? It is not difficult to understand why Berkeley itself is one of the main centers of such a movement. One factor is the university atmosphere; Berkeley has one of the highest academic ratings in the country. With 28,000 high-caliber students and some of the world's most renowned researchers and professors, Berkeley has status and prestige. In the pursuit of knowledge, Berkeley is where the action is. Added to this is Berkeley's reputation, going back to the Free Speech Movement in 1964, as a center for radical activities. These factors, coupled with the mild climate, nearness to the coast, and location in the cultural melting pot of the Bay Area, have made Berkeley an attraction for sightseers, political activists, runaways, pleasure seekers, outcasts, adventurers, and misfits.

But these considerations only answer the question "Why is the movement *here*?" and not "Why *is* the movement?" To answer the broader question requires looking to factors of a national and global scale that stand behind a place like Berkeley. It seems clear to me that we are living in the Age of Frustration and Despair. Man's need for security, for a sense of life's meaning, and for deep personal relationships goes unfulfilled in our age because of war, the threat of nuclear explosion, and the imminence of ecological disaster and population crisis. The tyranny of scientific methodology renders it impossible for many people to see the spiritual dimension of these problems. They are faced with meaningless lives void of self-identity. They have no inner harmony enabling them to cope with the turmoil of the world around them.

Nowhere that I know of is a better place to observe the effects of this malaise of spirit than the Berkeley street culture. In my view there are two major categories of street people. The first is those who live in despair, who have no hope at all. The second is those who are frustrated but who still have some hope.

Under the despair category are the Cop-Outs, the Pseudo-

Celebrationists, and the Societal Orphans. Cop-outs are those for whom nothing matters. They are completely irresponsible, unresponsive, bored, often spoiled, and disillusioned. They are hedonistic, living for immediate sensual pleasures and are characterized by the slogan "Do your own thing." A passage in the book of Jeremiah perfectly expresses their condition: "Turn back, every one of you, from his evil course; mend your ways and your doings. But they answer, 'Things are past hope. We will do as we like'" (18:11–12, NEB).

The cop-outs have lost all will to live responsibly; they are unconcerned about what is right and wrong. They are lazy and have interest only in those things which bring pleasure or excitement, such as drugs, sex, and riots. These are the most difficult people to reach. No longer interested in truth or meaning or content, they live for trips. Berkeley has many cop-outs. Smith and Alabama were two of them. Clipper, a heroin addict, is another.

The pseudo-celebrationists are also cop-outs, but they are more subtle about it. Deep down in their gut they feel that life is meaningless, that all is hopeless; they have given up just as certainly as the cop-outs. But rather than admit defeat they muster up a false affirmation of life, a false celebration. "On that day the Lord, the Lord of Hosts, called for weeping and beating the breast, for shaving the head and putting on sackcloth; but instead there was joy and merry-making, slaughtering of cattle and killing of sheep, eating of meat and drinking of wine, as you thought, Let us eat and drink; for tomorrow we die" (Isa. 22: 12–13, NEB).

Pseudo-celebration is affecting a surprising number of students, professors, and even some theologians. At a time when we should all be taking life seriously and taking God seriously, they have "tossed in the towel" before the game is over. They've given up. They are going through the motions of living, affirming what to them is absurd. They, too, are living for the present, often immersing themselves in drugs and sensuality.

The societal orphans are those who are not acceptable or not able to function in a society like ours that demands rigid conformity. Included in this group are psychological misfits and the insane, members of motorcycle gangs, runaways unable to conform to home or school expectations, and unemployed ghetto youths and Vietnam war veterans who find it difficult to establish a niche for themselves. Although most of the societal orphans are outcasts, unacceptable through no real fault of their own, some of them have become what they are by their own decision. My heart bleeds for those oppressed by social forces beyond their control. Mark and Tim are good examples.

In the second major category, the frustrated but hopeful, are the Revolutionaries, those who advocate return to the simple life, and those searching for higher meaning in the transcendent realm. Berkeley is undoubtedly primarily noted for its radical leftist politics and its revolutionary activities. Most of the sincere revolutionaries I have met are completely "this-worldly" as opposed to "otherworldly." They do not take seriously man's spiritual dimension and his need for spiritual fulfillment. Their belief is that man is determined by the social order. If the social order is corrupt or unfair, then man is a corrupt product of that order. If the order could be perfected, if everyone had equal opportunity, if everyone's material needs were satisfied, then all would be fulfilled. "If the present power structure could just be destroyed and replaced by us good people," they reason, "everything would be okay."

By projecting the guilt of the world's woes entirely onto the "Establishment," the revolutionaries allow themselves the illusion that they are guiltless. The self-righteousness of the revolutionaries blinds them to their own faults and allows them to believe that, if they were in charge, things would be better. They are for democracy only if they themselves are a part of the majority; if not, then democracy is no longer of any use to them. Sam is a good example. So is Blue, though she is motivated not so much by hatred as by the need to put into action what she feels is right. Another example is a guy named Darrell. His whole family became radicalized when his brother was clubbed and kicked at what started as a peaceful demonstration on a university campus. I saw pictures of his brother getting beaten. His father went to talk with the judge about his son's case after he was sentenced to jail, but the judge refused to discuss it. Darrell isn't interested anymore in democratic procedure; he's doing what he thinks is right. He sees revolution as the only means to secure a just society. What he fails to see is that violence brings about its own injustices and evils and that an oppressive minority is certainly no better than an oppressive majority.

Not all revolutionaries, however, are violent in their approach. In fact, I feel certain that a large majority of the University students here in Berkeley are opposed to the use of violence, though they share some of the same goals as violent radicals, including withdrawal from Vietnam, the end of racism and other injustices, and effective action to avert ecological disaster. If "revolutionary" is defined to include anyone seeking drastic changes in the structure and priorities of the nation, then most of these students would identify themselves as revolutionaries with a nonviolent approach to bring about change. They want either to work through the system, as Ralph Nader does, or nonviolently to challenge the system in boycotts and, when necessary, in civil disobedience as practiced by Gandhi and Martin Luther King. I have a great deal of hope in these people. They recognize the need for change, and they are willing to do something themselves to effect that change, although most of them lack an awareness of the spiritual need of man.

Berkeley has a large number of persons frustrated with the complexities of our modern world. They seek to live simply, in harmony with nature and man. Among this group are the flower children, who have been trying unsuccessfully to spread peace and love, and the craftsmen, including candlemakers, leather-workers, artists, flower salesmen, and wood carvers.

Making their own goods, the craftsmen sell them to passersby, tourists, and students in the small plaza outside Cody's Book Store. I've met one leather-worker named Condon. He is from Texas, is an expert in music, and is very well-read in philosophy.

Groups of people in Berkeley are seeking the simple life through living together in the same houses, pooling their resources, and living cooperatively as large families. Unified Family, founded on the teachings of a far-out Rev. Moon in South Korea, is one such commune.

Though this return to the simple life can be a good thing for the individuals involved, it obviously has its drawbacks. If everyone decided to do it, the complexities facing us today would never be dealt with. It is much more fun to live simply; but, with the survival of the human race at stake, a return to the simple life becomes unrealistic and, in most circumstances, irresponsible.

Adding to the variety of life-styles in Berkeley are the ever-increasing numbers searching for meaning in the transcendent realm. Our culture has been preoccupied with pragmatic values, order, the priority of respectability over authenticity, and materialism. The sterility of such preoccupation to the exclusion of deep feelings and relationships has caused the pendulum to swing to the other extreme. Now there is a profound search for meaning, for mystical experience, and for knowledge of the realm of the supernatural. Astrology is one avenue of this new interest. Others are the rise in Satanic cults, spiritualism, witchcraft, transcendental meditation, hallucinogenic drugs, Hare Krishna chants, Buddhist sects, and the Jesus People.

In contrast to the revolutionary elements in Berkeley, who are completely "this-worldly," these groups are "other-worldly." Their hope for life is found in the realm beyond, the realm of the spiritual. Some of these groups are terribly sinister and dangerous, particularly the Satanic cults, witches, spiritualists, and drug religions like Timothy Leary's L.S.D. cult. Others, such as Hare Krishna and transcendental meditation, apparently are helpful to some individuals in their attempts to quit drugs, get themselves together, and find something to believe in. Often, however, these movements are so otherworldly that they are of no practical value for living responsibly on this earth, here and now. Hare Krishna people, for example, spend a great deal of time chanting and giving out incense. In no relevant way are they related to the social, political, ethical, and economic problems of our day as far as I can see. Few people have nothing else to do but sit in the sun and chant all day. Meditation may do great things for the individual, but it doesn't acquire justice for the oppressed or feed hungry people.

The Jesus People should be separated from the rest of these groups. Many of them do tend to ignore the responsibilities of the Christian faith in this world, such as social involvement and dependability. In spite of this, however, they are definitely a source of great hope for the Berkeley situation. It seems clear to me that their movement is unquestionably the work of God. They are becoming a powerful rival of violent revolutionaries in attracting community interest. They are proclaiming the truth and are bringing lonely and lost human beings into contact with the living and loving God through the person of his Son, Jesus Christ.

33 · Christian Answers

August 21

Man is both culprit and victim. In biblical terms, man is a sinner, separated from God and at variance with God's purposes. Sin is self-defeating, both temporally, i.e., here and now, and eternally. The wages of sin is death. Sin is more than actions; it is a power that binds us so that we cannot do what we know we ought to do. It perverts our minds, our wills, and our hearts. Sin's power is cumulative. The more one gives in to its power, the more powerful it becomes. When sin is exposed, it manifests itself in defensiveness, hostility, and rebellion.

The power of sin has become demonic in America. Idolatry of science, materialism, greed, hypocrisy, racism, hedonism, sexual impurity, laziness, irresponsibility, pride of nationalism and person, self-righteousness, murder, rape, theft rings, political and ecclesiastical corruption, alcoholism, divorce, prostitution, betrayal of the convenant to be one nation under God with liberty and justice for all: America has turned her back on God. "In God we trust" is stamped on our money, but we have made the tragic mistake of confusing God with the money his name is printed on. "America! America! God shed His grace on thee." We can no longer take America's beauty or God's grace for granted.

As a Christian, I have hope for the situation in Berkeley and in the nation. But my hope is not in the goodness of man. To look at the world and say man is basically good is to me the height of naïveté and ignorance. True, man has the capacity for good, but he has a great problem putting that capacity into action. His sin pushes him to evil. The Marxist view that once man's socio-physical environment is satisfactory, he will be happy, well-adjusted, hard-working, and good is an inadequate understanding of the nature of man. It makes man's sickness much more shallow than it actually is. Man's sickness lies at the core of his being, the point at which he is alienated from God, in whom is his only possibility for fulfillment.

Neither is my hope in technology, for technology is but a tool of man, and can be used for good or ill. Nor is my hope in a return to the simple life because that is not a realistic confrontation with the complex problems facing us today. And my hope is not in the escape to a mystical otherworldliness that is unrelated to life and its responsibilities here and now.

My hope is in the living God who has revealed himself and his will for us in the Scriptures and in the person of Jesus Christ. My hope lies in him and in the promise he made to us: "If my people whom I have named my own submit and pray to me and seek me and turn back from their evil ways, I will hear from heaven and forgive their sins and heal their land" (2 Chron. 7:14, NEB).

Jesus Christ came that we might have abundant life. When we reject him and his will, we choose death instead. He loves us enough to allow us the freedom to make our own choice. But he wills life: "As I live, says the Lord God, I have no desire for the death of the wicked. I would rather that a wicked man should mend his ways and live. Give up your evil ways, give them up . . . Why should you die?" (Ezek. 33:11, NEB).

The hope of Berkeley, which is a melting-pot of the personal and social problems of our nation and the world, is in Jesus Christ and in our freedom to respond to him, to give ourselves to him and be transformed by him, to obey him by loving God and our neighbor as ourselves through the indwelling power of his Spirit in unity with our spirits.

In global crises, the Christian faith gives us the responsibility to become involved, to do our part in the area of ecology, to promote and work for peace and justice and love among peoples and nations, and to share food and material things with those who don't have enough. It gives us strength and power from beyond ourselves to meet those crises. It gives us the realization that our efforts, done in behalf of Christ, are not in vain.

The Christian faith rewards the quest for meaning in life with real content. It declares that God and his self-revelation in the Bible and most perfectly in the person of Jesus Christ are the ultimate authorities of truth and life's meaning and that nothing —not science or philosophy or anything else—can determine a more consistent, accurate view of truth and meaning. And the Christian faith gives experiential as well as intellectual meaning to all those who invite Jesus Christ into their lives and seek to live their lives loving him and obeying him. The power of his Spirit in our inner being makes the love of God and the will of God vital experiences in our lives rather than just intellectual concepts. We know who we are and what our life is about, for we find our ultimate self-identity as children of God.

For broken relationships, the Christian faith offers reconciliation in love between God and man and between man and man. The capacity to trust, to love, and to relate meaningfully begins to come alive for the Christian. Life and its relationships take on a new authenticity and depth.

The Christian faith is not so this-worldly that it fails to recognize the ultimate need of man for God, which is his need for deliverance from the power of sin and death into eternal life. But the Christian faith is not so otherworldly that it escapes recognition of the importance of life here and now and of our responsibility to be involved *in* this world, while not being *of* this world. The Christian faith offers a hope that encompasses all of life. It includes hope for the fulfillment of all man's needs, for its source is the God who loves the whole man—body, mind, and spirit.

34 · I'm Twenty-Four and She's Seventy-Eight

August 23

I am head-over-heels in love with Sarah Miles, a woman who has become involved in our coffee house ministry. She is radiant; her smile is overwhelming, disarming, and enchanting; her eyes sparkle; and her face is aglow with the peace and joy of

God. I have no trouble remembering her name because S. Miles is close to Smiles, and no word I can think of describes her better.

She comes down to the coffee house two or three days a week, always bringing along with her a couple of pounds of coffee and sugar or creamer for the street people. Her love is all-inclusive. No person in her path has escaped her warmth, her mesmerizing beauty, and her heart-felt care and friendship. She doesn't talk much, but then she doesn't have to. Her mere presence is enough to demonstrate the reality of God's love in the world. I thank God every time I see her.

Only one factor mars our otherwise perfect relationship: she is 78, and I am 24. Woe is me.

35 · Joy and Tears

August 24

Cheyenne is out of jail! I didn't realize how much he was missed by all of us until I saw the response he received when he walked through the coffee house door. The whole place came alive with shouts of joy, hugs, embraces, slaps on the back, laughter, and even a few tears. Cheyenne is "home" again. He got out on his word that he would show up for his trial, which is set for mid-September.

Though outward appearances indicate it's the same Cheyenne we knew before, after talking with him I've noticed a change. He is more serious now, more restrained than he was a month and a half ago. His experience in jail has apparently taught him to think before he acts, and though he is just as friendly as he always was he isn't as heavily influenced by the attitudes of the other street people. As he told me, "I'm staying clean, man; I'm staying clean." He has also started talking about the possibility of continuing his education: "Clay, do you think there's a Bible school around somewhere I could go to? I really want to be a Christian minister."

That was music to my ears. God can use any experience, good or bad, to bring about the change he wills in the lives of those who love him. Cheyenne is my friend and my brother. I sense in our relationship a special unity and purpose; perhaps God will use us as a team someday. Out of sight!

36 · Confrontation in the Hall

August 26

Two weeks ago a policeman gave a warning to a motorcyclist who had made an illegal turn, and the incident touched off a chain of events in Berkeley that affected our summer program. It began on a Wednesday morning, about 3:00 A.M. After the warning, the policeman and the cyclist were rapping about different things, just passing the time. A young guy, about 22 years old, walked up and joined the conversation, commenting that things had been peaceful in Berkeley lately. After talking congenially for a few minutes, he pulled out a revolver and shot the policeman in the head, killing him. He then muttered something about a political rally held the day before, according to the cyclist who witnessed the shooting, and ran a block to his car and drove away.

The two days following the murder were tense days. Just walking down the street I could sense powerful tension. It was not static tension but was increasing, building up as a volcano does when it is getting ready to erupt. It was as if the day of reckoning was finally upon us all, and no one was able to meet it complacently. For myself I was really shaken by the murder. True, in many instances the police are unjustly oppressive. But I honestly find it difficult to imagine a worse form of oppression than premeditated, cold-blooded murder regardless of who did it.

The day after the shooting I went down to the runaway center. The tension manifested itself in almost unceasing talk of violence, hostile shouting and threats on others' lives. The usual hostility which is often irritating but bearable was replaced by all-out hatred. It was as if evil had become incarnate in many human beings and was driving them to a point where they were apparently no longer able to control themselves. A large number of people in Berkeley, particularly the guys, carry weapons, including guns but primarily knives and razor blades. When violence erupts there is no telling what might happen. People were carried away by tension and hostility after the policeman was shot. Not only could they not trust those around them; they couldn't even trust themselves.

After sitting in the runaway center in this explosive atmosphere for awhile, I felt myself being taken in by it. I felt like lashing out at anyone who opened his mouth. Somehow I gave way to hating and I had an eager desire to cram my fist down someone's throat. I became concerned about myself when I discovered that, try as I might, I couldn't shake this hate and desire to do violence. For a few moments I really wanted to let loose on someone.

At this point I left the church for my room with the realization that it was going to be a very difficult night at the coffee house and that I had to get myself together before time to work. I could feel my inner self in turmoil; I felt like a battleground between forces of good and evil. It was difficult to pray. My hostility was not directed at anything specific; it was the general hostility of the drunk Western gunslinger of the movies who shoots contemptuously at anything that moves. I paced the floor of my room as the battle continued. Gradually the hostility subsided and was replaced, not by a peace as much as by a blank or void.

I remained apprehensive about working at the coffee house that night. I was tempted to call the church and say I couldn't make it. But I decided that was a cowardly thought and a cop-out, so I decided to go on as usual, come what may. I began to relax, once more able to pray and once again aware of the presence and love of God. I left for work with a deep awareness that God was with me and cared for me, but that there was danger ahead that I had to go through.

Sure enough, things were tough when I got back to the church. I cannot recall when I've ever seen so many up-tight, hostile people. Sam was especially filled with hatred and seemed to be highly effective at spreading it. He, Smith, and Jack, another regular this summer, were particularly down on Satan, our summer kitchen supervisor. They said they didn't like the way he took advantage of his position to take extra food home with him. There was little point to the accusation because Satan didn't get paid a cent for the work he did all summer. Behind their accusation was the need for an object at which to direct their hostilities.

Sam was so filled with hate that I realized for the first time he could kill a person—any person—and probably feel no remorse. He had once told me he was like a river with sand on the bottom and that it would not be a good idea to stir him up. I saw deeply into Sam that night, deep into the being of a man committed to get revenge, committed to destroy. Smith was more tense and hostile than I'd seen him at any time since he became a Christian. He had recently been jilted by a girl he likes a lot, and he just had to take it out on someone or something. And looking at Jack, who is 16 but claims to be 20, who sulks and makes threats when he doesn't get his way, I remembered that he packs a barber's razor in his boot.

The situation was building up to a climax. Feeling helpless, but making an effort to cool things, I walked around through the coffee house, then back into the runaway center. Just then I heard noises in the hall, like someone kicking holes in the wall. I went out in the hall and saw Jack kicking the wall and asked what he thought he was doing. He sat down, folded his hands, and just looked at the floor. I asked him again and he said nothing.

Then Smith made another remark about Satan and the cooking staff while Sam talked about the racism of the church. By this time I was really getting ticked off. The church is amazingly good to let these guys use the place at all, much less put up with broken windows, theft, and threats of violence. It was their own fault if they couldn't keep their heads. Smith had just muttered something when I said, "It's no one's fault but yours; it's your fault."

That one little sentence, "It's your fault," brought the day-long crisis to its climax. Smith misinterpreted my meaning and thought I was saying it was his fault that Jack kicked the hole in the wall. As a drop of water falling into a full glass causes it to spill over, the moment I had sensed hours earlier finally arrived. Smith started screaming obscenities and threats like a madman; he came into the hall and started kicking the wall himself and then came toward me, "You------, I'm gonna jack your jaw up." People inside the runaway center flew out to see what was happening.

I had spent many hours with Smith. He had been my friend. He had accepted Christ a month or so before, but he had not really let go of the old way of life. He did quit drugs, but his violent nature still found opportunities to erupt. He stood in front of me now, all six feet four inches of him, ready for attack. He was no longer the Smith I knew but was a stranger with the cold, evil eyes of one ready to kill.

But something else was taking place. In a matter of 15 seconds God moved in and transformed the entire situation. I felt his Spirit come within me, giving me peace as I gazed into the eyes of this friend who was ready to destroy me. Our eyes met as he swore and moved threateningly nearer, fists raised and ready to strike. I was not afraid, but was filled with a deep excitement much like joy. I spoke softly explaining to him that he didn't understand what I had meant. I could actually feel his hatred as it moved in like a huge tidal wave before it breaks. God broke that wave of hatred; he smashed it. I felt it subside and become harmless. Smith's eyes became soft, and we knew one another as friend and brother once again. We got things straightened out. Smith wanted to clean up the mess made on the floor when Jack kicked the wall. I helped him.

The climax had been reached. God came into the scene and no one was touched. Things cooled off after that. Although there was still tension, it was decreasing well below the danger point. The next two nights the coffee house was closed, at my suggestion to the pastor, because of the damage and the loss of tempers. I felt that closing the coffee house would make a person think twice before he would put a foot through the wall again. It turned out to be a wise decision for there has been no more damaged property. The following week Smith plastered up all the holes. Sarah Miles paid for the plaster.

As I look back on that incident now, as well as others like it, I am amazed at God's blessings and his protection. As many times as I have been around violence this summer, as often as I have had to rebuke and to discipline, it's like a miracle that not even once have I been harmed. I have been threatened numerous times, looked at with intense hatred, but never touched. "Because he cleaves to me in love, I will deliver him; I will protect him, because he knows my name" (Ps. 91:14, RSV). Time after time I have trusted God and been delivered and protected. I have stood my ground, spoken my mind, and haven't had to compromise myself or my commitment to Jesus Christ. These and other things that have happened this summer have enabled me to overcome much of the fear of violence that

I had before. I am better able to trust God in every situation. I feel more open to him than before and know that he takes care of his own.

37 · Cheyenne's Impact

September 2

This week, with 400 college and seminary students, I'm at the Forest Home Christian Conference Center, in the mountains close to Redlands, California, attending the College Briefing Conference. When I found I would be able to come here, I asked Cheyenne if he wanted to come too. He said excitedly, "Yeah, you'd better believe I'd like to." I told him not to worry about the money ($45 for the week). I set out asking different church members for help, explaining the circumstances to them. In two days, with the assistance of the pastor and his wife and four other members of the church, we raised all $45.

On the 400-mile trip down from Berkeley, Cheyenne and I gave a lift to a Brazilian named Claudio, who was on his way back to school in Texas. We sang songs for 200 miles, stopping only for breath. We sang old hymns, new hymns, and popular folk songs; we even made up songs, most of which were about the saving love and power of Jesus Christ.

Cheyenne's impact on the students at the conference has been remarkable. One of only two black people here, six feet two inches tall, and still wearing the gold earring in his left earlobe, he is hard not to notice. Though many were at first a little apprehensive and hesitant to become acquainted with him, Cheyenne's contagious smile and warm heart quickly melted all the ice. He is by far the most widely known and probably the best-liked person at the conference. Cheyenne accepts everybody as brother or sister; he treats everybody the same. He befriends the lonely, those who don't seem to be in the spirit of things. Jesus is in him.

38 · Signs of Hope

September 3

Getting away for the conference has given me time to reflect on this summer's experiences. I see a number of possibilities emerging that give me hope for the Berkeley situation. One is a trend toward nonviolent methods to bring about change. The great majority of Berkeley students, like students on other campuses, are concerned about the lack of justice in our society, corruption in government and business, our destructive policy in Vietnam, and the perversion of priorities and values. Yet, they have come to the point of rejecting the tactic of violence, and I feel they will separate themselves from the violent radicals. I believe they will also separate themselves from the cop-outs and the drug culture, recognizing that cop-outs and acid-heads are part of the problem and not part of the solution.

Along with these social concerns, a widespread renewal of interest in ultimate questions about God, man, and reality is evident in Berkeley. At this point I place a great deal of hope in the Jesus People and other Christian groups. My hope is that, as the Jesus Movement matures, its adherents will recognize the need to put Christian love into action, to seek justice, to speak prophetically to our society as well as evangelistically. The otherworldliness of many Christians, the belief that Christianity applies not to all of life, but only to the realm of the spirit, has kept some concerned people from looking seriously at the Christian faith.

This tendency of some Christians to otherworldliness is attributable to the widespread belief that the second coming of Jesus Christ is at hand, that these are the last times. I myself see this as a likely possibility. But I believe the expectation of the second coming of Jesus Christ should in no way pull us out of the world, but should serve to involve us ever more purposefully and responsibly in the world. Jesus tells us we are to be ready for his return. Being ready does not mean dropping out and doing nothing. It means doing God's will up until the very last. In Matthew 24:40–41, Jesus talks about two men working in the fields—one will be taken with him, the other left behind. He talks about two women grinding at the mill—one will be taken, the other left behind. In both instances the person is working, carrying out responsibilities at hand. Christians are not to drop out, but are more vigorously to involve themselves in the responsibilities of life here and now. We are not to be so heavenly minded that we are of no earthly good.

Jesus, prior to his death, knew he was going to die soon. He knew his earthly life would be over shortly and he would be exalted and glorified as the Risen Christ. But he didn't stop healing, ministering to, and loving those in need. He didn't stop condemning injustice and hypocrisy. He did the will of God until the end. The will of God is not just something to *know*, it is something we must *do*. Being ready means *doing* God's will, not tripping around saying, "It's all over; praise the Lord."

If the Jesus People realize the ecological, social, and political implications of the Christian faith, there will be a widespread revival of Christianity and thus of creative spiritual energy in Berkeley and across the nation. Of course, this revival's success will depend upon the response given the Jesus Movement by the Establishment churches. The Establishment churches need the Jesus People. They need their sparkle and enthusiasm, the effectiveness of their witness and testimony, their bubbling joy, and their love and acceptance of all colors and life-styles of people. On the other hand, the Jesus People need the Establishment churches. They need the content of the Christian faith revealed in the Scriptures and traditions as well as their own personal, invigorating experience of the faith. Unless the two come together, the Jesus Movement may deteriorate into a passing emotional fad with emphasis on feeling rather than on content, and the Establishment churches will die a slow death by failing to thirst for the revitalization of faith that only openness to the Holy Spirit can give.

Along with these developments is an increased awareness by the straight community in Berkeley of the needs in the street culture. The Free Church started the ball rolling in 1967, beginning to feed, clothe, and find housing for transient youths. The Free Church began ministries that have been picked up and carried on by other groups and agencies. Then, in the fall of 1968, the Telegraph Avenue Concerns Committee was formed comprised of city government leaders, businessmen, street people, faculty, students, and clergymen. The committee studied the South Campus area and made recommendations to city government; their main achievement was giving Telegraph Avenue a face-lift by widening the sidewalks into a plaza-like area with trees outside the various shops.

Then, during the summer of 1969, a number of new services were born. One was the Free Clinic, which offers medical care, emergency first aid, and a program known as RAP (Radical Approach to Psychiatry). The Free Clinic has treated more than 50,000 people since it began.

Started at the same time was the summer program in which I've been involved at the Baptist Church. Begun by the church's pastor, Dr. Ray Jennings, it includes the Free Food Program, which has served between 200–500 persons a day this summer, and the coffee house, a place to relax, to play music, shuffleboard, or cards, and to rap; the coffee house provides a structure through which concerned "straights" can get to know the street people and understand their problems. It also gives Christians an opportunity to share their faith on a person-to-person basis.

In March 1970 the runaway center was set up to help meet the needs of a rising number of kids who left home. And just this past summer, a youth hostel was established at a racetrack called Golden Gate Fields. The hostel provides overnight lodging for $1. The need is obvious as 1,400 persons per month have used the facility since it opened.

Along with all these new services, a few churches in Berkeley are beginning to take active roles in street ministries, and most others are financially supporting the different programs. A relatively small number of church people are personally involved; however, there are hopeful signs that the number is rising.

These programs are not cure-alls. They provide primarily for the physical needs of the street people. My hope is that a widespread awakening of the reality of Jesus Christ will provide for their spiritual and social needs.

39 · Tempted by the Mountain, Called to the Valley

September 4

It's beautiful on this mountain. Green trees, cool water, no smog. Seeing so many stars in the sky I realize I had forgotten how vast this universe is. It's quiet and peaceful at the conference center, a refreshing change from the intense hustle and bustle of life in the street culture. Those around me at the conference for the most part are happy, well-adjusted Christians, not the drug-taking, guilt-ridden, love-starved, alienated people I've known this summer on the Berkeley streets.

I feel a temptation that must be similar to what the disciples of Jesus experienced on the Mount of Transfiguration. Peter and John were with Jesus, and they saw a vision of Jesus with Moses and Elijah; they saw Jesus transformed before their eyes from a man into the glorious, overwhelming, majestic Christ, his face shining like the sun, armed with all the power of God. They fell trembling to the ground, in awe of the love and power of God. They were revitalized, their faith in Jesus was strengthened. Peter and John made a mistake, though. They wanted to pitch tents and stay up on that mountain where life was beautiful, peaceful, and revitalizing. They had forgotten the sickness and the suffering of those down the mountain in the valleys, those in need of food and clothing, those oppressed and in need of justice, those thirsting for love, and those who needed to know their Lord Jesus. Jesus led them down the mountain into the valley. That is where he leads us all—into the valleys to minister to those whom he loves and for whom he died.

I've matured as a Christian person this summer. One thing I've learned is the importance of the Holy Spirit in the Christian life. The Spirit of God grew inside me this summer, enabling me to love more deeply, more intensely, and more unconditionally. I've learned to look past hair length and skin color into the eyes, past life-styles into the heart. The Holy Spirit's presence within me, I am convinced, had something to do with the fact that I was not harmed in any way this summer. The vibes of the Spirit are love, joy, peace, and acceptance. To the extent that I was filled with God's Spirit, my vibes contributed to harmony and warmth. God's presence within me was my shield. But his Spirit was also my sword. For it was his Spirit that gave me increasing boldness and power to witness to others about the love and power of Jesus Christ and the fullness of life he has to offer.

I have become more sensitive, too, in my attempt to live as a Christian in response to God's commands to love him and my neighbor as myself. I have become deeply distressed about the failures of myself and my Christian brothers and sisters to love our neighbors in concrete, practical ways. We have failed by our unwillingness to sacrifice our abundance so that others might have enough; by our ignorance and inaction in the problem of social and political oppression; by our irresponsibility and apathy in the area of ecology; by our lack of concern for those at home and abroad who are suffering in the prison of poverty, malnutrition, and starvation; by our tendency to act as if God's love is limited only to particular nations, races, and life-styles; by our failure to realize that every human life is equally valuable and sacred to God, and that it is sin for a Christian to treat some people differently because of race, political ideology, life-style, money in the bank, or political and economic power. When the summer began, this was head-knowledge. Now I feel it in my heart. I'm beginning to practice what before I only professed.

40 · Another Person

September 5

On my last day on the job in Berkeley I conducted a Communion worship service in the coffee house. At 8:30 P.M. people began trickling into the room which had been used as a coffee house all summer. The room was dark now except for the flickering light of candles. Cheyenne helped me set things up. We put together three of the large wooden wire spools we had used as tables all summer and put five candles on them. We arranged chairs in a semicircle around the three tables with a small aisle down the middle.

I had taped some music the day before and had prepared a

message to go along with the music. We bought an unsliced loaf of bread and some grape juice to use as the Communion elements. Earlier in the day I had put up a few signs around the food line area announcing the service.

I didn't know what to expect that night. It was widely known around the coffee house that I was a Christian, and I had shared, sometimes effectively, my faith in Jesus Christ. But I had never tried a service like this. I didn't know if anyone would show up, and, if they did, I didn't have the slightest idea how they would respond.

At 8:30 only about ten people were in the room. Others began trickling in and when I started the service at 8:35 over 30 were there; when it was over and the lights came on, about 15 or 20 more had come in. We had a little trouble getting some of the people to come in at first though. Some of the regulars, like Sam who is a committed atheist, didn't want to go to anything that had to do with religion. Others wanted to play chess or cards. A group of six or seven blacks came in playing Mr. Cool, and they resisted going in to the service for a while. But eventually everyone present except Sam came in and found a seat. Alabama, Smith, and Jack were there, with many of the other regulars and some who were not. Even Johnny from New York City came in, and this time he wasn't sharpening his razor, though he was snickering as if he were going to cause trouble. The pastor and his family and the other summer workers also attended.

Some were making light of the whole thing with chuckles and whispers before we started. But the lightness melted away when the service began. Except for my voice, you could have heard a pin drop. I could never adequately describe the service, for it is difficult to explain on paper the effect of the presence of Jesus Christ. Jesus Christ was there in person; he could not have been more real had he been physically visible. His Spirit permeated the room.

I organized the service in four parts. The first part was concerned with the loneliness, the emptiness, and the despair of life. I played two recorded songs and had the people listen to the words and evaluate their own lives as they listened. The first song was "Sounds of Silence." The second was "Hymn." After the songs, Cheyenne turned off the tape recorder, and I went back over the words. I painted a picture of loneliness and emptiness, a picture that was no stranger to most in the room. I spoke about the way people talk without speaking. We talk, we mouth words, I said, but we don't speak from the heart; we don't cry out, "I want you, I need you to love me." I talked about the way people hear without listening, how they hear the words of those around them but don't listen to the lonely cries under the words. We wear our masks, we play our roles, I said, afraid to reach out and love, afraid to bare ourselves as the little children we are and ask for what we really need.

Because the overwhelming majority of the young in Berkeley are concerned about social injustice, or at least give it lip service, I went on to talk about the words to the song "Easy to Be Hard." The song was especially appropriate, for it points out that there are those who care about the bleeding crowd and the oppressed masses, but who can't see the person right next to them in need of love and in need of a friend.

The next song I played was "Who Will Answer?" by Ed Ames. This one tied together the first and the second parts of the service. It starts with situations of futility, life's contradictions and despair, and then leads to the questions about the search for something that will make sense of it all. After this powerful song I talked about how we stumble blindly, searching. I talked about the lovers who were so much in love that all seemed beautiful, but then an empty feeling voided their love. I talked about the father of a child he will never see because he was killed on a foreign battlefield, and for what? And the man on the lonely ledge ready to jump and take his own life. I told them I had talked with two people who had tried to kill themselves, persons who had come to the coffee house in the past two weeks.

Why? What is there? We need something really meaningful to fill our emptiness, to overcome our despair. We search. Who will answer? Who?

The third part of the service began with "Jesus Met the Woman" by Peter, Paul, and Mary. Then I went back to the song "Hymn" and talked briefly about how it describes the empty words and worthless conversations in many of the churches. I said that unfortunately the song was accurate.

Then I talked about Jesus in the song by Peter, Paul, and Mary:

Jesus has probably been presented to you in many ways. This song presents him much the way he was, I believe. Here was a woman Jesus met at a well, a woman who didn't have much going for her. She had had five husbands, and the one with whom she lived now was not even her own. Jesus still loved her and accepted her. Though he didn't dig what she was doing, because she was destroying the possibility of her own fulfillment and that of others, he still loved her.

His life was one of giving himself to people who needed him. He spent most of his time with those who needed him the most—those sick mentally, physically, and spiritually and those lonely, lost, and in despair. A woman taken in adultery was brought to him. He loved her and because he loved her, he told her to "Go and sin no more."

The religious Establishment began to frown upon his activities. He spent much of his time with people who, in the eyes of the Establishment, were bad and unclean. They called Jesus a drunkard, a glutton, a blasphemer, and a sinner. They were eventually largely responsible for his death.

Jesus, the embodiment of perfect love and justice, was crucified in the most evil act of human history. We, the human race, took Jesus and we said: "God, this is how much we hate you," and we nailed him to a tree. And God looked down, his heart breaking, and said: "My children, this is how much I love you. I am going to use the death of this my Son, whom you have killed, to wash your sins away."

The song "O Happy Day" tells us that Jesus washed our sins away, that God transformed the worst act in history into the highest good.

Jesus Christ died on a cross about 2,000 years ago. There are those who say he rose. They say that the Spirit of God came upon the corpse of Jesus and raised him to life, and that he is the Christ, the Son of God. They say he is still alive, he is the Risen Lord, he loves now as he did then.

I believe with all my being that Jesus Christ is alive, not in a figurative way but actually. And I believe that he is here, present with us, in a very real sense.

The last part of the service was the Communion. I explained that, if we participated, we had fellowship with Jesus Christ as well as with each other. I challenged each person to think about the things he had heard. I challenged them to let their participation in this communion with Jesus Christ be for them a meaningful experience and commitment in their lives.

Cheyenne turned on the last song, "Let's Get Together and Love One Another," and then he assisted me in serving the bread and grape juice representing the body and blood of Christ to those who came forward. The song was perfectly appropriate, for there was a flood of love in that room which I have seldom if ever seen before. There were many tears, and lives were changed as the Spirit of Jesus Christ brushed by us and around us and through us.

The most amazing change was in Johnny; he was completely transformed. Usually very hostile and obnoxious, he became an overflowing source of love. Tears streaming from his eyes, he walked up afterward and hugged me. "Man," he said, "Wow, what freaky vibes . . . far out . . . Wow." He was overwhelmed by the love of Jesus, and it welled up within him like a spring of sparkling, pure, clean, living water.

Four or five of the black guys came up to see me too. When they first walked in the coffee house that night, they were wearing sunglasses, popping their fingers, playing the role that many of the black ghetto-dwellers play—Mr. Tough Guy, Mr. Slick. During the service the masks came down and they quit playing their roles. They became authentic people, sincere, gut-level, honest, and beautiful. One said, "Man, I mean, like you really spoke to me, you know what I mean, man? I mean, you came across. It was almost like I was saying the things you were saying; that's how real it was to me. You hit home, man. Thanks." Another black guy came up three or four times, thanking me, tears in his eyes: "If there's every anything I can do for you, let me know, okay? I mean it."

Jack, the 16-year-old kid who kicked a hole in the wall not long ago, was there. After it was over, he walked out without saying a word. He went to be by himself for awhile. He told me later: "That was really heavy, Clay. I got some flashbacks in there about things I've done that I shouldn't have. I'm gonna have to get myself together . . . No kidding, that was really heavy. Thanks."

Another person at the service, whom I'd seen some during the summer, works with one of the underground newspapers. When the service was over, he walked up to me, his eyes a little moist, and looked deeply into my eyes. He embraced me; then, without conversing at all, he walked slowly out the coffee house door into the night.

A guy with a reputation as a professing atheist walked around in a daze, apparently stunned by the whole thing. He kept muttering: "My gosh, my gosh. I never knew church could be like this." Apparently his grounds for atheism had been seriously shaken that night.

The pastor told me it was one of the finest things we'd done all summer and his only regret was that we hadn't tried it sooner. Gail, Donna, and Chuck, the other summer workers, were all deeply moved as well. So was Cheyenne. So were Smith and Alabama. So was I.

I was as amazed at what happened as every body else. I thanked them for thanking me and praising me. But it was not me, or the music, or the words that made the experience so overwhelming and so precious. That night we were honored with the powerful love that accompanies the living presence of another person, who is The Man, whose name is Jesus Christ. He blessed us. Our lives, the lives of all of us, were changed and enriched by his presence that night.

72 73 10 9 8 7 6 5 4 3 2 1